ABOUT THE AUTHORS

Author
Antoni Lenkiewicz

Born in 1934 in Ostrołęka, Łomża region, descendant of a Bar confederate who had served under Pulaski, and himself a Stalinist prisoner from 1952 to 19.., Antoni Lenkiewicz holds a doctorate of law and master degrees in history and philosophy from the University of Wrocław. One of the most active organizers of the Solidarność movement in the Lower Silesia, he served on its Board and participated in Solidarity's first nationwide convention. On the infamous night of December 13, 1981, preceding the imposition of martial law, he was part of 6,000-man mass arrest. Interned for a year he was arrested again in 1985 and kept in prison for nine months, to serve later, after the "round table" talks, on the City of Wrocław council from 1990 to 1994. Lenkiewicz has been a prolific writer and sought-after speaker and lecturer on topics relating to the Polish drive for independence. As a watcher of the current political scene, he has been publishing his monthly bulletin "Wrocławska Gazeta Polska" since 1994.

Co-author
Ted (Teofil) Kwiatkowski

The author's California friend, Ted Kwiatkowski is an architect and a graduate of the Technical University of Gdansk, a popular writer on the history of architecture as well as a history buff and portraitist. Born in 1920 and a prisoner of wartime years, 1942-1945, he wrote his memoirs, "My Serendipity," about the cosmic grace that allowed him to get through the vicissitudes of his time. He sees the same serendipity in Pulaski, a survivor, whose valor and courage made it possible for him to extricate himself from one bad situation until another throughout his short life.

Leszek Szymański (Introduction), editor, historian and fiction writer, author of "Casimir Pulaski. A Hero of the American Revolution." New York, Hippocrene Books 1994.

Regina Gorzkowska-Rossi, editor, literary and art agent, founder of Pro Arte Associates, was a patricipant in the Warka conference, "Casimir Pulaski in Polish and American Consciousness" (DIG, Warsaw 1998). Since 1997, she has edited Philadelphia's Pulaski Day Parade Supplemet, "Nowy Dziennik."

Antoni Lenkiewicz
Ted Kwiatkowski

FOR
YOUR FREEDOM
AND OURS
CASIMIR PULASKI
1745-1779

Introduction by Leszek Szymanski

BᵂT

Biuro Tłumaczeń
Wrocław 2004

Edited by Regina Gorzkowski-Rossi

Cover design by Victor Guirard

©2004 by Biuro Tlumaczen and Pro Arte Associates

Sponsored by Pro Arte Associates

ISBN 83-88826-29-8

For information, address:

B͞Y̆ Biuro Tłumaczeń
50-550 Wrocław, ul. Wieczysta 77/33, Tel./fax 48 71 336-70-44
E-mail: gazetapolska@poczta.onet.pl

Pro Arte Associates
1801 Buttonwood Street, Suite 1513
Philadelphia, PA 19130, U.S.A.
E-mail: proarterg@yahoo.com

Printed in Poland

Prepress – Studio **TArt**, Wrocław
Press – Drukarnia **REPR●**, Wrocław

CONTENTS

LINE MAPS

Poland 1770

Casimir Pulaski's battle trail in America, July 23, 1777 to October 11, 1779. After Zdzisław Sułek, "Polacy w wojnie o niepodległość Stanów Zjednoczonych 1775-1783" (Warszawa 1976).

Battle of Brandywine, Sept. 11, 1777. Taken from "The Pictorial Field-Book of the Revolution" by Benson J. Lossing (1860).

Battle of Germantown, October, 1777. Taken from "The Pictorial Field-Book of the Revolution" by Benson J. Lossing (1860).

Siege of Savannah, Oct. 9, 1779. Taken from "The Pictorial Field-Book of the Revolution" by Benson J. Lossing (1860).

ILLUSTRATIONS

Group portrait of Bar confederates with Casimir Pulaski in the middle. After "Album of the Bar Confederacy" by S. Wolski (1899).

Joseph Pulaski (1704-1769), Casimir's father. Unknown painter. After Władysław Konopczyński's "Kazimierz Pułaski" (Kraków 1931).

Karol Wettin, Prince of Courland. By an unknown artist.

Francesca, née Krasińska, Princess of Courland. By M. Stein.

Printed after Władysław Konopczyński's "Kazimierz Pułaski," Kraków 1931.

Casimir Pulaski and Confederates by Częstochowa. Oil by Juliusz Kossak.

INTRODUCTION

*P*ulaski's name once rang heroically in the New World and in the Old. Now, its resonance lost, it is just another foreign-sounding name in the cacophony of the American city and highway lexicon. Dr. Antoni Lenkiewicz's book re-establishes its validity for the general reader by explaining why Pulaski became a legend.

This biographical sketch is written with an understanding and sympathy for Pulaski's life, truly a tale of conflicts and drama. Many blank spots remain to this day in his life. Dr. Lenkiewicz fills them with the talent and rich imagination characteristic of his writing. The author's sympathetic attitude permeates the entire story.

Though officially recognized by the Communist authorities of the bygone era in Poland, Pulaski was a troublesome hero for them. A nobleman who had sacrificed an enormous fortune, social position, career and, finally, his young life, for liberty and republicanism, surely, Pulaski was a role model on the scale of Marquis Marie Joseph LaFayette. Yet, he was also a leader of the Bar Confederacy—the first Polish anti-Russian insurrection, and of a fanatically Catholic character, to boot. Thaddeus Kosciuszko, Pulaski's contemporary and companion in the American pantheon of heroes, though also a leader of another anti-Russian insurrection, was easier to swallow. Kosciuszko was a Democrat, peasant-lover, and, by origin, a member of petty gentry. Dr. Lenkiewicz's book on Pulaski, entrenched in his strong opinions, not shunning controversy, countered an official interpretation and could not pass the censorship of the bygone era.

Incidentally, it was Kosciuszko, and not Pulaski, who became the main hero of Polish immigration in the United States of America, mostly peasant in origin. In Poland, Pulaski—a supreme master of guerilla warfare during the long and harsh years of staggering difficulties and in face of an overwhelming enemy force—was the soul of armed resistance. He could fight as well from behind the walls of besieged cities, as to lead the regular infantry and cavalry triumphantly. His defense of Częstochowa brought him worldwide fame. More, he had gained an enormous experience as a quartermaster and trainer of raw troops in war conditions.

He was a superior horseman, a military genius, strategist and tactician. What he was not, was a politician. Because of that, he suffered disappointments both in Poland and in America. After the fall of the Bar Confederacy, Pulaski appeared on the side of rebellious American colonists. He was granted, albeit reluctantly, the command of a nonexistent cavalry. Accordingly, he created the cavalry from scratch, rightfully deserving the name of its Father. Then, because of professional jealousy and intrigues, he was forced to leave that powerful war instrument only to see it wasted by his successors. Despite these drawbacks, he did not desert the American cause. He proceeded to organize an independent legion, and continued his struggle for American freedom.

In America as well as in Poland, Pulaski achieved the optimum. In both countries, he is remembered in the folk tradition as the Knight of Liberty. Dr. Antoni Lenkiewicz gives us a concise and clear-cut handbook on Casimir Pulaski's life. For anyone interested in learning more about the hero, Lenkiewicz's compact guide will remain a signpost for future study.

Leszek Szymanski, Ph.D.

FOREWORD TO AMERICAN EDITION

*M*y special fascination with the two heroes of Polish history, Joseph Piłsudski and Casimir Pulaski, dates back to a "child's world" which—a poet asserts— stays with us forever. The portraits of the two Marshals, as they were referred to, hang at my parents' home in Ostrołęka, Łomża region in Northeast Poland. Childish inquiries about the pair would invariably evoke a positive response, deeply affecting the child's imagination and consciousness. It took me years to fully grasp the difference between the marshalcy of Piłsudski and Pulaski. It was important to me that my earliest historically documented ancestor, the first to settle down in Ostrołęka, arrived from Lithuania where he had served under Casimir Pulaski. As his subordinate, he participated in Pulaski's proclamation as the Marshal of Łomża.

In studying Polish history and writing about it, I was aware that there was no chance for publishing any honest and unbiased research on Joseph Piłsudski under the political situation then. I might have been overly optimistic and perhaps even a bit naive, but I felt that a book on Casimir Pulaski could have a better chance of appearing in print. I dedicated time, energy and creative effort to achieve that end.

In the mid-1960s, with the bicentennial of the Bar Confederacy approaching, my manuscript was ready. I submitted my study on Pulaski to several state-owned publishing houses, one after another. Some in-house reviewers actually liked it, remarking it was well written but suggested significant revisions to which I could and would not consent. It dawned on me that, although Pulaski was not as dangerous as Piłsudski to the Soviet rule in Poland, what was essential in his life, pertaining to his national and Catholic viewpoints and anti-Russian and pro-American outlooks, could not pass muster without omissions and adulterations.

5

The 1980s were the boom time for popularizing the historical merits of Piłsudski and Pulaski. It was not because the authorities relented with the birth of Solidarity and loosened their grip on the society. Rather, that information was in demand by many Solidarity activists and could be disseminated by the so-called "second circuit" of underground publications. During my confinement as a political internee after martial law was declared in December, 1981, my perennial topics as a lecturer were, on the one hand, the Bar Confederacy with Pulaski as a leader and, on the other, the Polish war against the Bolsheviks under the command of Joseph Piłsudski, head of the Second Polish Republic and Commander-in-Chief of the Polish Army.

I commented on my two heroes in a stream of articles. My books went into several editions and were occasionally aired by Radio Free Europe. My biographical book on Casimir Pulaski was reprinted by Toronto's Polish Canadian "Gazeta" in 1988-1989, and the Polish National Alliance's daily newspaper, "Dziennik Związkowy" in 1991. Published covertly in Poland, these works fell short of quality standards. I recommend only the revised and amended fourth edition, appearing in 1999, at the 220th anniversary of Pulaski's death. This formed the basis of the current American edition.

Antoni Lenkiewicz
Wrocław, March 15, 2004

THE HERO OF
THE TWO NATIONS AND ONE CAUSE:
INDEPENDENCE

*T*he fame of historical figures and knowledge of the deeds they accomplished to make them famous do not necessarily go hand in hand. Casimir Pułaski is a handbook illustration of this. With Thaddeus Kosciuszko, he heads a list of Polish participants in the American War of Independence. Unfortunately, this is about all the public knows about Pulaski.

Pulaski has rarely been a topic of objective discussion and scholarly research and publications. One does hear boisterous, if repetitive, rhetoric about his heroism for immediate political consumption. Epithets and half-truths are hastily concocted to provide "factual data" to back the rhetoric. Pulaski research tends to be colored by a researcher's politics. Forces averse to Polish-American cooperation not infrequently tried to inveigle that our Polish heroes were underestimated in America. The Bar movement, which had produced Pulaski, was presented as a suspicious string of events and an example of Polish sedition and mindless Catholicism which had pushed Poland to the brink of the first partition.

The duality of opinion on Pulaski is an overgrowth of the general trends in thinking on the evolution of Polish history, from the 17th century until now. Those who are critical of Polish uprisings, Catholicism and Polish opposition to Russia could not and did not look favorably upon the "hero of the two continents." Those who do see the importance of fighting for "our freedom and yours" put him, quite naturally, high in the pantheon of champions.

Casimir Pulaski lost his life while fighting for independence in the United States. He embraced the American cause as a continuation of his struggle for independence in his own country. As the Colonel of the Confederacy, Marshal of the Łomża region, and the

Brigadier General of the American cavalry, Pulaski served the same ideals and was faithful to the same cause.

His particular contribution was that he had grasped the immensity of the Russian threat to Poland and Europe, and he dedicated his whole life to resisting that threat. He opposed Russian expansionism primarily as a Bar confederate, a regimental leader of guerilla warfare, the defender of Berdyczów, the Holy Trinity trenches, and Częstochowa. At the peak of the Confederate uprising against the Russian rule in Poland, 1770-1771, he was one of the most popular commanders and a candidate for Commander-in-Chief.

At that time Russia realized that she could neither swallow nor digest Poland without outside help. She sought allies. Prussia and Austria, under any pretext, were eager to participate in breaking up Poland. Nevertheless, the two were concerned about public opinion and needed arguments to validate their action. Masters of international intrigue and blackmail, Russia tried to undercut the Confederate movement, accusing it of intolerance and anarchy. In 1770, the specialists of the tsaritsa's propaganda machine devised an effective ploy. The provocation that deceived almost everyone was a coup d'état against the ruling monarch, King Stanisław August Poniatowski. Sparing no effort or expense, they started a smear campaign against Casimir Pulaski across Europe declaring him an "inspirer" of the coup and, as such, guilty of "regicide," and sentenced him in absentia to death for the assassination attempt. Until the present, historians kept reiterating that the Confederacy's greatest blunder was its attempt at the king's kidnapping. As one alleged: "the involvement of the [future] hero of the American War of Independence blurred somewhat the clarity of the paragon's biography." The matter will be discussed further in these pages. It may be mentioned here that the kidnapping was actually done by two individuals, Stanisław Strawiński and Kuźma-Kosiński. Both most probably acted in the service of Moscow, since they were neither captured nor punished but generously rewarded by the Tsaritsa and the King himself. Shortly after the declaration of the Third of May Constitution (1791), when the pressure of the Russian Embassy in Warsaw momentarily relented, the Polish Seym fully vindicated Pulaski and his sentence was revoked.

The list of writings on Pulaski is quite substantial. Still the best books among those written in Poland, even though slightly outdated and wordy, are: "Żywot Kazimierza na Pułaziu Pułaskiego" ("The Life of Pulaski of Pułazie") by Leonard Chodźko (Lwów 1869) and "Kazimierz Pułaski—życiorys" ("Casimir Pulaski—His Life Story") by Władysław Konopczyński (Kraków 1931), a source of our quotations. The books on Pulaski, published during the Communist period (Jan Brzoza 1960, Ryszard Zieliński 1967, Karol Koźmiński 1968, Jan Stanisław Kopczewski 1979 and Janusz Roszko) are all, in general, garbled and dictated by the pro-Russian and anti-American politics of the period.

American authors who wrote on Pulaski were, to name a few: W. W. Gordon, Mieczysław Haiman, C. A. Manning, W. H. Richardson, J. Sparks and W. Wayda. In the 1990s, two works were published in the USA: "Casimir Pulaski: A Hero of the American Revolution" by Leszek Szymanski and "Casimir Pulaski, Soldier on Horseback" by David R. Collins. These two books focused entirely on the two years of Pulaski's service in the American Continental army, omitting his military career in Poland. They seem to underscore, in general, American disinterest in what Pulaski did in Poland and Europe. Szymanski's book is a monographic study in depth of Pulaski's stay in America. Almost literally for the first time in a century, after W. Kozlowski's 1905 "Pulaski in America," the author revealed unknown or little known documents and facts, and he shed new light on Pulaski's difficulties in America.

That book is scholarly. I would like to mention briefly that it disclosed Pulaski's conflict with General Washington over the role and usage of cavalry, the weapon unknown in America. Pulaski gained the respect and support of two of Washington's opponents, Generals Charles Lee and Horatio Gates. Some of Pulaski's tactical ideas were rejected even though, had they been introduced, they would have shortened the war.

Most writers on Pulaski disregarded the period 1745-1767, preceding his participation in the Bar Confederacy. However, in order to understand fully Pulaski's dedication to the idea of independence, one must learn the background of his early life leading to the Confederacy and his later involvement in America. We need to study what had shaped his character and political direction. Without understanding those circumstances a text on Pulaski would bog down in descriptions of audacious exploits and adventures, skirmishes, battles, victories, and defeats, with no understanding of his real drive and valor. The only moral reached would be that "a great warrior he was" but, perhaps, without clear motivation, one equally confused in his politics and mocked by the circumstances as many other heroic soldiers. Think of the Polish September of 1939 or of the Warsaw Uprising. Or, on the American scene, think about the soldiers of Vietnam.

In all his public actions, Pulaski manifested his supreme dedication to "God, Honor, Freedom and Independence." It is significant and revealing that he attached so much importance to "independence" although its Polish usage prior to the Bar Confederacy did not have its current political connotations.

Pulaski's contribution to Polish history is much greater than to U.S. history. He was the first to point to the legionary way "For Your Freedom and Ours" as a means of regaining independence and was also the first to die for "Your Freedom and Ours," becoming the symbol of exceptional sacrifice, faith and heroism. The mortal wound at Savannah, on October 11, 1779, ended his life at the age of 34. Had he lived longer, he would have been needed, at the age of 46, in the fights to preserve the 1791 Constitution.

That did not happen. For consolation, though, let us remember that his patriotic struggle had not occurred in vain. His presence in the pantheon of Polish and American fighters for independence may help us keep in mind our mutually shared values and common battles for their attainment.

PROVERBIAL HAVOC:
FROM "LAS" (Leszczyński)
TO "SAS" (Saxon)

*T*he Pulaskis of Pulazie who bore "Ślepowron" (literally 'Night Heron,' though Casimir prefered to use 'Corvin') as their coat-of-arms were a noble family of ancient lineage, thoroughly Catholic and Central Polish (despite their cherished but undocumented tradition that they had arrived from Lithuania, united with Poland within the Polish Commonwealth). Historic records trace their origins to the early 15th century, with the first mention dated 1435. The next record, dated 1537, referred to the family estate Pułazie (from which their name was derived) being subdivided into Pułazie-Grochy, to be inherited by the sons of Szczęsny (Felix) Pulaski and Pułazie-Gołębie to go to the sons of Marek Pulaski. Over the generations, they were forced to "forge ploughs into weapons."

In 1555, when Tsar Ivan the Terrible attacked the Courland, Poland's fiefdom on the north, Maciej Pulaski distinguished himself among defenders and envoys. His swift action saved the land for Poland. In 1621, Captain Rafał Pulaski headed his own hussar regiment, which listed his 10 sons, against the Turks at the battle of Chocim. The Pulaskis took part in the defense of Częstochowa against the Swedes in 1655. Colonel Wojciech (Adalbert) Pulaski fought, in 1658, under the command of Hetman Stephan Czarniecki and crossed with him to Denmark to pursue the retreating Swedes. Simon Pulaski, in 1683, fought the Turks at Vienna with King John III Sobieski.

The Pulaskis' military record underscores their involvement in public affairs. Francis Pulaski, who died in 1738, left it for his son to publish his "Brief Annotations of the Warsaw and Grodno Seyms." Pertaining to the history of the Polish legislative body from

11

1648 to 1733, the book covered the elections and coronations of four kings: John Casimir, Michael Korybut Wiśniowiecki, John III Sobieski, and August II the Saxon. Francis's brother, Stephan, had supported Stanisław Leszczyński, nicknamed "Las," against "Sas," Augustus II of Saxony, who was backed by Russia for the Polish electoral throne. Stephan, the grandfather of Casimir Pulaski, was killed in 1709 in the battle of Kalisz. His son and Casimir's father, Joseph Pulaski, was five years old at the time. Joseph (born 1704) scarcely remembered his father and was raised and educated by his mother, Margaret. Joseph was a man of remarkable abilities. In 1731, Joseph, who was adept with a pen, had a politician's smooth tongue and a background in the humanities, became a successful, high-ranking lawyer of the tribunal in Piotrków Trybunalski. Actively supporting, in his father's wake, Leszczyński's claim to the Polish throne, Joseph Pulaski took his regiment from Czersk to Dzikowo (now part of Tarnobrzeg) and fought in several confrontations with the Saxon forces. However, when the campaign failed, he was reconciled with the elected Saxon. On October 7, 1738, Joseph married Marianna Zielińska, of the Świnka crest, related to senatorial families of Mazovia and Kujawy.

At that time, the powerful Czartoryski family initiated a reform movement called "The Familia." The term implied both the Czartoryski clan and their political party. Joseph Pulaski, colonel of the hussars, marshal of the Polish army, and an extremely wealthy landowner who owned 108 villages and 14 towns and cities—was a vociferous, though not uncritical, supporter of the Familia. His voice was especially heard during the 1744 Seym.

After many interrupted sessions, that Seym opened with a new hope for achieving long-overdue reforms of the army and treasury needed to modernize and strengthen the weakened Polish Commonwealth. The patriotic atmosphere was quite hopeful. General Stanisław Poniatowski, father of the future king, circulated an appeal to electors entitled "Letter from a Polish Nobleman." Joseph Pulaski, an eloquent lawyer, campaigned with him for a patriotic common sense. Representatives of the lands and parties were jointly behind the reforms. This bothered the Russian and Prussian diplomatic observers, who attempted to derail the reform movement. After weeks of honest deliberations, the debates became twisted. The Czartoryskis and Potockis, at first working together, split into two hostile camps. Controversies and mutual accusations marred the final turbulent five-week sessions. No breakthrough was reached. When the Seym closed on November 19, 1744, nothing of consequence was enacted.

Failure of the Seym to pass the urgently needed fiscal and military reforms in the face of the subversive actions of Russian and Prussian agents resulted in a shift in the politics of the Familia, now willing to try to save the sinking country with Russian support. That proved to be in vain, for counting on Russia was equivalent to trusting a hungry wolf to merely lick a wounded lamb.

CASIMIR-MICHAEL-VACLAV-VICTOR

asimir Pulaski was born in those turbulent times, "from Las to Sas," in 1745 as the middle of Joseph's three sons. He also had six sisters. The record of Casimir's christening was recently brought to light by Władysław Rudziński who, while searching for his family records in Holy Cross Church in Warsaw, discovered an entry in the Register of Births dated March 14, 1745. This record noted that Kazimierz (Casimir) Michał (Michael) Władysław (Ladislaus) Wiktor (Victor), son of Joseph Pulaski and Marianna from the Zielińskis, was baptized on that day by the priest, Father Krzysztof Falz. His godparents were the leaders of the Familia: Stanisław Poniatowski, father of the future king Stanislaw August and Voivode of Mazovia and Princess Maria Zofia (Mary Sophie) Czartoryska, Ruthenian Voivodine. The Czartoryskis and the Poniatowskis had their residences near the church and the Pulaskis' mansion was close by, on Warecka Street. This Registry entry supported Warsaw's claim to being Casimir's birthplace, and not Warka, as was believed earlier.

Casimir's childhood may safely be supposed to conform to what we know from numerous memoirs from the period concerning the typical Mazovia gentry, except we would have to consider his father's wealth and interests in the humanities and politics. The list of books perused undoubtedly did not lack "New Athens," Father Benedict Chmielowski's almanac, imparting his Saxon-time wisdom to the general public. The family collected consecutive "Volumina Legum," a serial publication on Polish laws, started in 1732. They would have definitely treasured "A Free Voice Assuring Freedom," published in 1749 by ex-king and philosopher Stanisław Leszczyński from his retirement in France who presented his politics in the hope of being re-elected.

Throughout his childhood, he would have traveled between the country residence in Winiary near Warka and their Warsaw residence. His father was a "Starosta" or District Magistrate of Warka. Their stately country house there, designed by August Locci, presently houses a museum. The grounds feature a huge statue, erected there in 1979 by American Poles to commemorate the "hero of the two continents." The bulk of time, undoubtedly, he spent in Warsaw because of his father's juristic and political engagements as well as his father's sincere concern about his children's education.

While young Casimir was growing up, his father Joseph, opposing any kind of dependence on Russia, left the Familia movement and joined a new program created by the great Polish patriots, Jan Klemens Branicki and Stanisław Konarski, called "The Republicans."

Young Casimir was brought up in the knightly tradition. At the age of five he began his horseback riding lessons. As an eight-year-old boy, he owned his first Arabian thoroughbred. In those early years, the future cavalry officer mastered fine horsemanship. Casimir was educated in a superior institution of learning, Collegium of the Teatinian Priests in Warsaw. Why was his education not at the progressive Collegium Nobilium? Perhaps because the College was financed by the Czartoryskis. The Teatinian College enjoyed an equally good reputation. The school had educated Stanisław Poniatowski, the future king, 13 years Casimir's senior, well known for his love of arts. Education at the Teatinian College was conducted on an individual basis. Each student had his own teacher, a censor who was a grader, and one or two "calefactors" or helpers. Apart from math and physics, logic, dialectics and metaphysics, and, of course, Latin, they were taught modern languages: French, Italian and German as well as elocution and oratory. Attention was paid to good manners, eloquence and skill in public affairs as well as— a new subject—Polish history. Casimir had an opportunity to learn dancing and the art of letter writing.

The Teatinian fathers implanted the highest values: honor, chivalry, dedication and devotion to his homeland. One of the prominent teachers was Anthony Maria Portaluppi, who organized the school theatre where Casimir played the role of Julius Caesar. We know this from Casimir himself. In his defense when accused of the king's kidnapping, he mentioned the knightly rules he had learned at the Teatinum and his part as Julius Caesar in a school play. Professor Portaluppi propagated the modern philosophy of Wolff (now entirely forgotten) and Cartesian teachings. Young Casimir liked school and was a good student but he preferred military games, horseback riding, fencing and pistol shooting to reciting Latin verses.

Casimir enjoyed spending vacations in his country residence, Warka, with his elder brother, Frank, especially bravado horseback riding or riding in the Pilica river, skirting a ruined castle that was once the residence of Mazovian princes. They spent much time in the Kozienice wilderness, playing hunting games and enjoying the pains and delights of being close to Nature.

According to the Jędrzej Kitowicz's description in his memoirs, Casimir was of slender posture, and though not tall, he was physically strong, fast in speech and movements when walking. He mentioned his card playing which was probably part of a teetotaler's social persona.

It is believed that in 1759, while attending the wedding of his sister Joanna, Casimir met Francesca Krasińska, a very attractive young lady of a prominent family. Although, they both were very young, our hero began paying her parents increasingly frequent visits, and fell into platonic love with her. Francesca, too, was fond of her distant relative and enjoyed sharing youthful friendship with Casimir. They attended dances together, and took part in carnival balls for aristocratic youth in Warsaw. At that time, her unusual charm enchanted another very handsome young man, Karol Christian Joseph, who was the son of King Augustus III and Mary Josephine, daughter of Emperor Joseph of Austria.

Karol had just received the Kettler crown as the Prince of Courland. He was witty, wore elegant French attire, liked Poles, and distinguished himself by his happy and vivacious manner. All these, and the prospect of becoming Princess of Courland, maybe even the future Queen of Poland, made sixteen-year-old Francesca disregard obstacles and accept Karol's proposal.

On November 4, Karol's nameday, the wedding ceremony took place without the king's consent, at Węgrów, Mazovia. A priest from Warsaw celebrated the wedding, with many potentates in attendance. The secret marriage was soon made public, but attempts to dissolve it were unsuccessful. Through all that, Francesca remained on friendly terms with Casimir. Legend says that she was his only lady-friend throughout his lifetime.

King August III, in spite of Russian opposition, appointed his son, Prince Karol, to govern the Courland, which was under the Polish protectorate. Casimir Pulaski joined the journey to Courland. He stayed on as Karol's page in Mitau (Mitawa, now Jeglava), in present-day Latvia, for several months. The position, in the traditional courtly training, was meant to bring about the final gentlemanly polish, and it taught him an additional lesson in politics.

The situation at the Castle of Mitau was difficult. Several battalions of Russian troops stationed there were a source of tension. Prince Karol did not have enough troops, nor had he strong hand nor a clear head. The Russian commander, Simolin, virtually controlled the city.

Aside from the usual hunting and practice shooting with a pistol, Casimir's six months at Mitau gave him an insight into the forthcoming war with Russia. Mature beyond his years, he became proficient in Russian. The angry Tsaritsa Catherine II, determined to incorporate the Courland, pressed August III to recall his son from that outpost. Her diplomacy failed for the law and the support of the Courland population was on the king's side. Prince Karol had only a small garrison of Polish troops in Mitau. To depose him, the Russian Empress sent more troops to Mitau. Courland's knights and Polish youth firmly resisted. Day by day, tensions were rising. Weeks passed and the Russians increased their violence. They blockaded the castle where Karol's garrison was headquartered and terrorized town inhabitants.

Despite the arrival of a Polish detachment commanded by Commissioner Plater, the Russians, on February 15, 1763, broke the castle gates and robbed the castle treasury. Local resistance was too weak. Constant pressure from Moscow forced King August III to capitulate. He recalled his son. in April, 1763. The greatly disappointed Poles were commanded to leave the outpost.

Sad experiences of Russian brutality convinced Karol and Casimir alike of the Tsaritsa's aggressive intentions toward Poland. On the way back to Warsaw, they were talking about returning there, some days later, with adequate power.

When in Warsaw, Prince Karol, without much display of regret for his lost Duchy, resumed his frivolous life style. He did not care much any more for his young and pretty wife. Casimir returned to his family-owned Winiary where he reverted to his preferred practice of war games, horseback riding, fencing and wrestling. It was a hush time before warfare began.

ELECTION OF THE PIAST

*I*n 1752, at the Seym of Grodno, King August III tried to have Francis Xavery, his politically well versed son, elected—"vivente rege" meaning during the king's life—as his successor. This would curtail electoral monarchy and assure a dynastic continuance of the Saxon house.

Polish patriots supported his idea as a good chance for recovery of the Republic. Russia and Prussia, mixing more and more in Poland's internal affairs, were firmly set against it. Also, the Familia opposed the Saxon succession, hoping that candidacy to the Polish throne might go to someone from the Czartoryski clan.

On October 5, 1763, after 30 years of a rather peaceful reign, King Augustus III Sas died in his hereditary Saxony, in Dresden. In view of his demise, all parties expected serious changes to come about. In the period of interregnum that followed, the Poles became convinced about the need of breaking with foreign dynasties and electing a king of Polish stock to the Polish throne.

The Electorate claimed for a candidate from among the Polish nobility, or a "Piast," so after a successful native dynasty that ended to give way to the greatness of the Jagiellons. Frederick of Prussia and Russian Empress Catherine II, much against the opposition of the conservative Polish aristocracy, supported, under the pretext of defending religious rights for dissidents, the election of a "Piast."

At that time, Familia losing support because of their leaning toward the Russians, proposed General Adam Casimir Czartoryski as a candidate to the Polish throne. On the other hand, the Republicans in the persons of Prince Jan Klemens Branicki, Prince Radziwiłł "Panie Kochanku" (dubbed so for his habit of inserting 'Darling' in his speech), Bishop Kajetan Sołtyk, the Krasińskis and the Pulaskis supported the continuance of the Saxons on the Polish throne. From among August III's sons, Prince Karol Wettin would be their choice even though Karol was not keen on becoming king.

Then Russia and other Polish neighbors had different ideas. Ignoring all this, the Russian Empress Catherine II, the Great, made a decisive move. She proposed, and supported by force, the candidacy of a commoner, General Poniatowski's son, Stanisław August. A Pole from Lithuania, he was known as a "golden youth" in St. Petersburg and was at one time the Empress's passionate lover.

Regardless of the opposition from the Republicans and other parties of discontented Polish magnates who had to suffer the defeat of their candidates, the election took place on August 29, 1764. With the Russian army protecting the Electoral Seym, Stanislaw August Poniatowski, the later popular "King Staś" (pronounce Stash), became King of Poland. A festive coronation ceremony was held in Warsaw, at St. John's Cathedral, departing from the tradition of coronations in Cracow's Wawel Cathedral. The ceremony was attended by most of the Polish nobility, including Joseph Pulaski who, accompanied by his sons, must have had mixed feelings. Stanislaus August was dressed with all appropriate regalia in a royal vestment of his design. Mixed in the crowd, Casimir Pulaski listened to the king's patriotic invocation: "Merciful God, whose will was to give me this crown, let the voice of my appeal and the passionate desire to save our Fatherland reach You. Lord, complete Your work and pour into the hearts of the entire nation the love of the Country, such as I possess."

Like others in attendance, Casimir wondered if these words were sincere. Initially, the election, dictated by Russia, was considered in the Polish circles to be a misfortune though some parties viewed it as a useful measure for displacing the somnolent Saxons from the Polish throne. Although dependent on Russia, pliable and cosmopolitan, the new king, to everyone's surprise, turned out to be an ardent patriot and convinced reformer. At that time, no one had a premonition of the pending catastrophe of the Polish state. Carl Keyserling, a Prussian diplomat in the service of the Russian empress, arrived in Warsaw in support of the new king. He became quite cooperative and friendly with the Czartoryskis. Then watchful

Russia sent an all-peremptory supervisor, Prince Nicholaus Vasile-
vich Repnin, who was well provided with a sizeable army, and an
armful of bribe money, promises and threats. He practically dictated
his will to the Poles.

Prussia decorated the newly elected Polish king with the order of
"Black Eagle" and Russia with the order of Andrei Pervozvanyi,
both supreme state distinctions. On April 11, 1764 Russia and
Prussia signed an alliance in favor of the Polish King to grant him
support, assurances and guaranties. For the time being, Familia took
a neutral position. The Republicans were in opposition but their
attempts mattered little in view of the powerful Russian army heading toward Warsaw, allegedly to protect Poland from growing anarchy and to keep the "law and order."

Persuaded by the Familia, a well-respected statesman Władysław
Alexander Lubieniecki called for a special Seym to convene in
Warsaw on May 7, 1764. With Senator Andrew Mokronowski,
backed by 22 senators and 46 envoys objecting, the previous speaker, Adam Małachowski, refused to open sessions unless the foreign
army left Warsaw. In that situation, the Familia decided to open the
sessions in the name of the Confederation, and they nominated
Adam Czartoryski as the Seym Speaker. Emotional discussions prevailed amidst hot, patriotic arguments, but no firm decision was
reached except for a manifesto. After protesting the presence of foreign armed forces the Confederation departed from Warsaw in
protest. A civil war threatened to break out in Poland.

Casimir was then 19, at the threshold of adulthood. To be some-
body, one had to hold a public office. His father appointed him
"Starosta" or Elder of Zuzuliniec County in Podolye. Most of the
time Casimir was residing and working in the country's periphery,
near the Russian-Turkish border. Living there, he came to the con-
viction that to regain total independence, a war with Russia was
inevitable. To win this war, the conflict between the two big powers, Russia and Turkey, was of the utmost importance.

Meanwhile friction between the parties was replete. Nevertheless,
opposition was growing. More and more voices demanded that the

foreign armies leave the Polish territory. Russia and Prussia voiced their support of religious minorities to assure them equal rights with the Catholics. This gave them an entry into the country's interior politics. Obviously, they were meddling not for reasons of religion but politics. The undecided king was caught between a rock and a hard place. This made the angry Russian ambassador conspire for his impeachment. Repnin moved through the Seym a bill conferring equal rights upon dissidents, Russian Orthodox and Protestants alike, throughout the Polish Commonwealth. It was meant to deal a blow to the supremacy of the Catholic Church and inspire resistance. The cunning Repnin outmaneuvered the distraught nobility mobilized in the defense of the church. Some fell into his trap and formed a Confederation at Radom to fight the new law.

CONFEDERATION OF RADOM

*I*n 1767, when Casimir was 22 years old, more and more new Russian troops were entering the Polish territory, allegedly to end anarchy and restore order. In reality, their goal was to stop any further attempts at reforms necessary for preserving Poland's sovereignty. To achieve their policy, Russia and Prussia tried to organize the so-called "Dissidents' Confederacies" in Lithuania and in Poland proper, in Słuck and Toruń. This way, they tried to eliminate the Polish struggle for independence by making the Poles sidetrack themselves.

The plotting Repnin toyed with the idea of the King's dethronement. He promised the dissatisfied conservatives, craving for the return of the "good old Saxon days" with their "golden freedom," to satisfy their wishes and replace the King with a more amenable person. Many of them swallowed the bait and joined the Confederacy of Radom which was set up by the Russian ambassador Repnin. However, Hetman Klemens Branicki of Białystok, with Joseph Pulaski in the group of his allies, did not trust the Russian and refused to cooperate with any Russian endeavor.

In Radom, electors assembled in the city hall, surrounded by the Russian artillery, with guns pointed at the windows. Then, the Russian commander Colonel Karr declared:

Primo: "The King must stay as King."

Secundo: "The King's Government may only be improved by way of amendments, with no return to the old and bad government."

Tertio: "This Confederacy will be merged with those from Łuck and Toruń and will be considered as one unit."

Quatro: "That nobody shall leave the building until all sign the pledge of allegiance to this Confederacy."

In this way, Confederacy of Radom, turned out to be Repnin's political success. Prussia was pleased as well. In July 1767, a delegation from Radom arrived in Warsaw. The King was shocked. The Czartoryskis' position had weakened and the opposition got stirred up and set at variance. As the Confederation of Radom was coming to a close, the arrogant Repnin and Joseph Pulaski, twice his age, clashed physically. The older was pushed and kicked in the presence of the King, who apparently remained indifferent.

This incident spurred the 64-year-old lawyer Joseph Pulaski, burning with a patriotic fervor and angry to boot, to form a new Confederacy, unlike the Radom Confederation. He had on his side individuals like Bishop Kajetan Sołtyk, Great Hetman Jan Klemens Branicki, Field Hetman Wacław Rzewuski, Prince Karol Radziwiłł, Bishop Adam Krasiński, Michael Krasiński, Paul Mostowski, Frank Potocki and others. This opposition knew the armed resistance was unavoidable.

Casimir Pulaski was sent to Prince Karol Wettin with the mission of winning his favor for the insurrection. Repnin responded first with threats of assassinating the "troublemaker" Bishop Sołtyk, followed by a threat of the church breaking with Rome and establishing an independent Church of Poland.

The night of October 13, 1767, Russian soldiers kidnapped two bishops, Sołtyk and Zamoyski. Protests from Czartoryski, Zamoyski and others were ignored. From that time on, the opposition became clandestine and Joseph Pulaski was chosen its leader. Although hounded by the Russians, he was lucky to spend the Christmas of 1767—his last one—with his family in Warka.

At he beginning of the year 1768, Joseph Pulaski traveled to Lwów (Lviv) for an important meeting with Archbishop Sierakowski. Then, in the middle of January 1768, the secret order, Knights of the Holy Cross, was established, counting among its members the majority of ardent Catholic Polish magnates. They were against the principles of the Radom Confederation. The swearing-in took place in the historic Holy Cross Bernardine monastery in Lwów with all the due ceremony.

The next meeting for the public declaration of the new Confederacy was planned at Kamieniec Podolski. Remaining loyal to his King, the commander of that fortress refused to go along. He arrested conspiring officers within the fortress and declared martial law.

In that situation, a pious little town of Bar in Podolya was chosen to be the seat of the upcoming Confederacy. The town was unfortified and indefensible, so to speak, but in a good location. The Reverend Marek Jandołowicz was building a monastery at Bar, and the Pulaskis owned a number of villages, among them Nowosiółki, in its vicinity.

CONFEDERACY OF BAR

*O*n February 29, 1768, a consortium of disillusioned Polish nobility, headed by Michael Pac, formed the new Confederacy. The consortium was composed of the Potocki, Sapieha, and Krasiński clans. An official Act of Confederacy was convened and written down, and the oath-taking ceremony was conducted in the Carmelite monastery at Bar in the most earnest, lofty and solemn words. "In the name of the Fatherland, the Holy Catholic Faith and Liberty, it is hereby resolved that the Radom Confederacy and the Warsaw Diet (Seym), whereas acting under foreign patronage, are illegal."

In order to validate this resolution, because of the necessity of armed resistance against the Russians, further decisions were reached. First, to create a strong army, by recruiting young men from all over the country and putting them under the command of sworn-in Knights of the Holy Cross. Secondly, to make an appeal to all citizens who loved the faith and the country, to get on horseback and join the Confederacy. No Protestants, Calvinists and other dissidents need apply. From each of 10 peasant huts, one soldier was to be drafted. Each commander was obliged to own two horses, a pistol, a sword and a banner. He had to wear the sign of the cross on the left side of his body and a four-corner cap with a fur band and without a hood. This type of cap, "konfederatka," was used in later insurrections and became a symbol of patriotism. Troops were to be organized into hundred-man units headed by colonels. Three Pulaski brothers, Frank, Casimir and Anthony, were assigned this rank.

On March 4, 1768, or the day of St. Casimir, who was a Royal Prince of the Jagiellon dynasty and the patron saint of the Polish-Lithuanian Union, the new Confederacy was established. The inauguration ceremony included solemn Mass with an eloquent sermon by Father Marek Jandołowicz, acclaimed as a prophet of the movement, who repeatedly castigated Russian hypocrisy and violence. A festive military parade, with flags and banners, drums and trumpets, followed the Mass. Like other commanders, Joseph Pulaski's attire glittered with gold and jewels. Casimir Pulaski wore, Hungarian fashion, a green jacket with golden buttons and had golden spurs and an embellished saber and pistols.

Legend says that the white eagle soared above the troops and headed west. Joseph Pulaski, the newly appointed Commander-in-Chief of the entire army, delivered a patriotic address. All the colonels pinned symbolic "Pro fide et liberte" (for faith and freedom) medal on their left breast. Messengers were sent to all governments and magnates, Pope Clemens XIII, King Stanisław August Poniatowski, the Grand Vizier and Sultan, Empress of all Russia Catherine II, carrying special envelopes sealed with the Polish coat-of-arms and carrying an inscription: "aut vincere aut mori" (either win or die). The new program called for a temporary limitation on unnecessary fighting. Most actions were directed at building up the armed forces, collecting weapons and ammunition, fortifying castles and waiting to be prepared when the Turks awoke and struck against Russia.

Happy with such a propitious beginning, the confederates ended the remarkable and eventful day with a big fiesta, accompanied by military music. During the first few days, five other units joined the Confederacy and more followed. It was, indeed, a good omen for the movement. Many Russian peasants attempted to escape to Poland, where the living conditions, compared to those in Russia, were, they claimed, an "oasis of justice." Encouraged by such an attitude, the Confederates issued an appeal to Russian soldiers, calling for mutual solidarity in the joint fight against the Russian-German despotism.

At the same time the Council of the Polish Senate in Warsaw initially condemned the Russian lawlessness, but after a hot debate, concluded that "blowing against the wind" would be useless and decided to take action against the Confederacy. They sent General Mokronowski to negotiate with the Confederates. They also turned to the Russian Empress for military help to suppress the rebellion. Moscow responded immediately by sending a special penal expedition complete with infantry, artillery and hussars totaling up to 8,000 well-trained troops, headed by General Peter Krechetnikov.

For the poorly trained Confederates, the confrontation with such an enormous army in the field would be disastrous. The only way to deal with them was the "hit-and-run" tactical warfare in which Casimir Pulaski proved a master. He gathered in his unit more than a thousand men and, as the regimental colonel, he won several "hit-and-run" battles with Kretechnikov's overwhelming forces.

Maneuvering of that sort proved successful, and Casimir grew in skill. His tactic was to confuse and disorient the enemy. A simulated attack was followed by a sudden withdrawal, leading the enemy into a trap. Then, he encircled the entrapped and hit them with a swift cavalry attack. On one occasion, in a bitter battle at the village Kaczanówka, Casimir was wounded in his right arm but bravely beat the Russians with the help of his artillery. Conducting this kind of warfare, by playing those kinds of war games, the confederates were gaining time in anticipation of the big war between Russia and Turkey.

With this war in mind, the Confederate staff decided to occupy some of the forts on the Polish-Turkish border and fortify them to encourage the Turks to act against Russia. The fortress of Kamieniec Podolski, the most significant border stronghold, seemed to be the right place to begin. But again, loyal to the King, its commander-in-chief, General de Witte, refused to give it up to the Confederates. To take this citadel by force remained only a wishful dream.

In spite of their patriotic persuasion, the confederates met with similar resistance from the garrisons of Biała Cerkiew and Kaniów. The General Staff of the Confederacy moved from Bar to Winnica located 40 miles southward and continued to undertake limited actions, making preparations for the big war to come when they would fight side by side with the Turks. Negotiations with the Turks were about to begin. Frank Pulaski was dispatched as an envoy to friendly Pasha Benderowski. Stephan Makowiecki was sent to the Sublime Porte, Constantinople. Casimir Pulaski had the honor of welcoming a delegation of the Grand Vizier at the border. The two parties, exceptionally festively dressed as the custom dictated, met at the bank of the River Dniester. With the sound of drums and trumpets from both sides, they first politely exchanged greetings and salutes using courtesy French.

Then, they all proceeded to Winnica for a reception and negotiations. Mediations with the Turkish envoy were hopeful, but the upcoming events were not favorable for the confederates. Joachim Potocki, one of the powerful magnates who joined the Confederacy with 5,000 well-trained and armed militia, was defeated terribly on his way to Bar. He became discouraged and moved to a safe place in Turkey. In addition, Russian troops flooded the Polish Republic.

Following Krechetnikov, another Russian general, Apraskin, marched into Poland. The King's army under the command of Ksavery Branicki stood by the Russian side. In support of Bar, several new, secondary Confederacies rose nationwide in Lublin, Bracław, Podhajce, Stanisławów, Buczacz and Halicz, but, in fact, they all were powerless.

The Russians came up with an even more effective weapon—they resorted to plotting intrigues. They provoked anti-Polish riots among huge masses of Russian Orthodox peasantry. Acting on promises of privileges, the peasants exploded with grand-scale merciless slaughters of Poles, Jews and Catholic clergy. The so-called "Hajdamacs" were headed by two Cossacks: Maksym Zhelezniak (generously rewarded later by the Russian empress) and Ivan Gonta, who infiltrated Poland from the East. For the confederates, facing the riots was more dreadful than confronting the overwhelming Russian army. In the face of the world's opinion, Catherine II, of course, denied any Russian involvement. Waves of murders, carried by those "Hajdamacs," encompassed most of the Ukraine sinking the countryside in blood. To stop the riots, the royal army joined forces with the Russian army to come to the rescue of the population.

One of Russian colonels, pretending to be sympathetic to those "Hajdamacs," invited their leaders, Zhelezniak and Gonta and others, for a seemingly friendly meeting. There was a big party abundant in food and with drinks for everyone. On the next morning the "Hajdamacs" awakened in shackles and without questioning, they were all mercilessly killed.

BERDYCZÓW

*A*part from the Poles and the Russians, Turkey remained on the war arena. The Russo-Prussian alliance worried other European countries but they did nothing to counter it. When queried, Russia persistently denied any interference in Polish internal affairs. The Tsaritsa's propaganda machine came up with a naive explanation that her army heading toward Warsaw was nothing more than an escort for a delegation coming to celebrate the Polish King's nameday, a counterpart of a birthday celebration in the Catholic country. Only Russia could afford a grand escort of 50,000 troops! That was difficult to believe but equally difficult was getting credible information from outside source–British and Prussian envoys in Poland supported the Russian claim that they just had several thousand troops in the country.

Young Casimir Pulaski embarked on his military career as a recruiting officer, raising troops and gathering supplies. Growing in experience and military skills, he developed tactics of guerrilla warfare, which he employed with great success. Yet the situation of the Confederacy was critical. The force of about 4,000 confederates was not unified, but scattered throughout the territory. A decision was reached to stop the Russians advancing under General Krechetnikov at the fortified Berdyczów monastery. Casimir Pulaski was chosen to take the command of the fortress at the head of some 1,400 confederates.

The springtime of 1768 was in full blossom when Casimir Pulaski defeated a Russian battalion under Major Ploetz and, with a great deal of enthusiasm, proceeded to Berdyczów. He found the city quite defensible: its dry moat was bisected by a high and strong wall and a gate—

a single point of entry—slanted to better resist the enemy's gunfire. The bridge leading to the gate could be drawn in. A battery of cannons in good working order protected the only gate. The foreground of the stronghold was taken up by relatively strong buildings and the fortress was backed by an extensive marshland and the river. An old and respectable Carmelite monastery, treasuring a miraculous painting of Our Lady of Berdyczów, was within the city walls.

The Russian General Krechetnikov arrived with 5,000 troops, well supplied and equipped to lay a siege. When he inspected the fortress ahead of his staff, Casimir Pulaski greeted them with a fire of his artillery but on the next day he sent out an officer with a flag of truce. He referred to the Slavic unity and assured that the confederates were neither against the Russians nor the Orthodox faith. Casimir promised that nobody would bother the Russian army returning to their own land. It is highly unlikely he expected his negotiations would result in a breakthrough but his politicking was gaining him time since his primary goal was to distract Krechetnikov from Żytomierz where the Kiev voivodeship was convening to join the Confederation.

The Russians broke negotiations and for several days kept the fortress under fire and then announced an attack to take place at the dawn of May 31, 1768. On that final night Pulaski, ahead of 200 volunteers, organized a sally to confuse the attackers and to lay their assault plans into disarray. The wounded included General Krechetnikov's cousin, Michael. Taking advantage of the rule of the series, he organized another sally the very next night. That night the confederates let loose horses, not needed in the fortress. Men with torches of straw and tar followed the galloping frightened animals. Amidst the fires and horses dazzled with fright a fierce battle broke out aimed at taking and destroying Russian cannons. Pulaski repeatedly resorted to provoking overnight battles but, in view of the Russian superiority, even when fully successful, they were merely morale boosters and had propagandist effect.

The situation in the fortress grew more difficult as food and ammunition supplies were running low. The Russians managed to cut off water supplies. The last monastery cannon went silent on

June 3rd and the enemy prepared to enter the city gathering fascine, rearranging ladders and tying them together, and threatening the defenders with a total annihilation. Pulaski was under a growing pressure to surrender since the expected relief was not coming and news reached them that it was defeated on the way. Finally, the bombarded fortress could not respond and went quiet. Carmelite monks and some honorable citizens pleaded with Pulaski to negotiate respectable conditions and capitulate. Pulaski was compelled to lay down his arms on June 13, 1768, two weeks after the siege had begun. Sadly, the desperate capitulation took place just shortly after Krechetnikov, blamed by Commander-in-Chief Repnin for wasting ammunition and making no progress, received his orders to withdraw.

The relieved and happy Kretechnikow received the Polish submission with a great deal of pleasure. From that joy, he promised good treatment of the confederates and of the townspeople. Then he proudly reported to Repnin his victory and did not forget to gratify himself with ample booties from the monastery treasure and safety deposits.

Despite the given guaranties (Casimir demanded them in writing), Kretechnikov detained Casimir Pulaski and several members of his staff, and sent them to a prisoner-of-war camp for confederates in Płonne. A week after the capitulation of Berdyczów, the city of Bar was seized by the Russian forces under General Apraskin accompanied by the Polish Royal units. The Confederate movement was expanding and growing stronger but from within the confines of the prison it appeared to be the end. More and more prisoners were coming to Płonne, where Casimir and his brother Anthony were confined, and where Father Marek Jandołowicz, a convent priest and an inspiration as a prophet of the salvation of the Fatherland, suffered misery.

Was it an end of their fight against the Russian supremacy? Were they now facing a prospect of a Siberian exile and hard labor which was a prolonged death? He knew about the Siberian exile, first used by Peter the Great against King Stanisław Leszczyński's obdurate supporters and what General Siennicki reported from Siberia in his memoirs published in 1754. Now he was listening to the sinister sound of "kibitkas" departing eastward and was consumed by helpless wrath witnessing much abuse and maltreatment of those prisoners who rebelled and requested their rights honored, men being stripped naked and severely beaten.

Meanwhile, King Stanisław August Poniatowski, under the pressure from his uncles from Familia, obtained Empress Catherine's consent to amnesty those prisoners who would sign a declaration of loyalty, called "recess." Most likely Ambassador Prince Repnin himself, acting on the King's behalf, requested the Tsarina's pardon for "the son of Warka who cut such a gallant defense of Berdyczów." Most probably, the King's sentiment for his father's godson motivated Stanislaus Augustus to plead for Casimir's freedom. Repnin expected Casimir would respond to this magnanimity when he wrote to Krechetnikov to authorize him "to send him [Casimir] on his way to join his father and the rest of the troublemakers."

Casimir was released from the Russian prison on July 17 and was on his way to Chocim and Turkey, where his father and other leaders of Confederacy were planning their next move. If Repnin did in fact count on some kind of appreciation on Pulaski's part, he was mistaken. Casimir considered signing his "recess" of loyalty to be a means of saving his head and, with a clear conscience, decided to revoke it at any time. In his next letter to General Kretechnikov, Repnin ordered him to inflict the hardest rigors on Pulaski, if caught again.

In an open manifesto, Casimir Pulaski declared that his signing of that piece of paper was made null since it followed upon Kretechnikov's broken promise of letting him and his officers go free after their capitulation. In view of this fact, Casimir explained, he felt no guilt after breaking his obligation toward Krechetnikov, and he wrote that he (to quote the letter) "sincerely and honorably declares that he will never betray his Fatherland neither his father's creed, nor the Confederacy." "I am aware," he wrote, "that death awaits me when recaptured by the Moscovites, and I prefer to look for my death on the field of glory fulfilling my duty to the nation. I did not feel bound by my signature even for a moment and they will never again get me alive."

The constantly growing confederate troops consisted mostly of cavalrymen–young boys on horses—unprepared to resist the well-trained columns of Russian infantry. In order to conserve its strength, the Confederacy decided to move from Winnica, the new headquarters of the confederates, further east, behind the River Dniester to the Turkish side and remain there until the time came for Turkey to strike against Russia.

In October, Casimir received his father's permission to return to Central Poland to commence once again gathering supplies and ammunition and enlisting new recruits. Soon after, Joseph himself reentered Poland to reorganize the Confederacy.

CONTROVERSIES AND INTRIGUES

*D*espite partisan politics and charged competitiveness over top leadership undercutting unity so urgently needed at that crucial time—the Confederate army got reorganized. In August 1768, two divisions were established. The first one was the Ukrainian division under command of Joseph Pulaski and the other one, under Joachim Potocki, was called the Podolyan division. An influential personality, General Joachim Potocki— that rank he received in the foreign armies—considered himself to be the best qualified for the position of Commander-in-Chief for both armies and he sought to remove Joseph Pulaski from his post. A realist as ever, Pulaski made a politically wise move and on September 11, 1768, he voluntarily ceded his command to make it possible for Potocki to step in.

The takeover did not go as smoothly as expected. Since almost the entire Confederate command took refuge in Turkey, many old animosities arose there among the Confederate elite. There were also significant differences of a tactical nature. At that time Joseph Pulaski was not excluding the possibility of allegiance with King Staś and he continued to urge for immediate action without waiting for the Russian-Turkish war to break out. His strategy was to enter the Central Poland territory and continue fighting oncoming Russian units in support of armed regional confederacies to push the Russians out of the country. "To bring the entire army into the Cracow Voivodeship," he argued, "will help our brothers to realize their strength." The Potockis and the Krasińskis had different ideas: they saw the need to get firmly established prior to embarking on the premature hostilities, "not to dissipate our strength in vain."

Back in June, while chasing the confederates, a Cossack unit encroached on the Turkish territory. As a consequence, on October 6, 1768, Mustafa III, in the name of the Sublime Porte or Ottoman Turkey, declared war on Russia in support of Poland. Joseph Pulaski had long waited for this moment and without hesitation began his program of immediate action. He entered the Polish territory with all his troops, ready for action. His proclamation read: "This is the time awaited by the Polish nations long oppressed by power and perfidy and eager to defend faith and liberty."

Gathering at Żwaniec, the confederates debated how to renew the Bar Confederacy and made changes in commanding personnel. Because the Commanders-in-Chief Joachim Potocki and Michael Krasiński were still in Turkey and not contemplating an immediate return to Poland, the temporary high command in charge of the Confederacy was given to Marshal Wawrzyniec Szeliga Potocki. Joseph Pulaski was in support of this move. Michael Krasiński, feeling dismissed from the command, issued a proclamation, most likely consulted with his brother, Bishop Adam Krasiński, wherein he used his authority to remove Joseph Pulaski from command, piling all kinds of slander on him. Shocked by the scandal, the Tartar Kierym Girej, under a pretext, invited Joseph Pulaski to come to Chocim. Then, following the plot of the two titular commanders, the Turkish authorities had him interned.

Meanwhile, Casimir Pulaski, his brother Frank, Wawrzyniec Potocki and Maurycy Beniowski, were fighting a guerilla war on the Pulaski lands near Zuzuliniec and Mohylew, east of Zaleszczyki, successfully hurting Russians. Princess Francesca lived at that time at Bishop Krasiński's residence at nearby Dunajowice. Casimir had a chance to meet with her and visit his old flame.

At one time, Casimir's guerillas intercepted royal mail with a personal letter from King Stanisław August Poniatowski to General de Witte, commander of the fortress Kamieniec Podolski. In his letter, the King commanded not to yield the fortress to the Russian allies but keep it exclusively in the Polish hands. This news of the King's true thinking raised hope in Pulaski's heart of having the King mend his ways to serve Poland. Unfortunately, Repnin's wrath and a threat of impending dethronement made the King align himself with the worst part of the Senate to turn to the Russian empress for more troops against the confederates. Despite this decision, King

Stanisław August Poniatowski did not yield to Repnin's persuasion this time, and largely refused to use the Royal Army against the confederates. At that time, the Polish king also refused Catherine's request to use his troops in Russia's war with Turkey.

Their field of maneuvering becoming more and more limited, the Pulaski brothers, with a small unit of faithful soldiers, installed themselves in two fortresses: Żwaniec and Okopy Świętej Trójcy, or Holy Trinity Trenches, at the mouth of the Zbrucz discharging to the Dniester River. When Repnin dispatched General Izmailov with 4,000 men to take these two fortified towns, Frank held Żwaniec with 400 soldiers and two cannon, and Casimir guarded Holy Trinity Trenches with 350 soldiers and six cannon. On March 8, the Russians launched simultaneous attacks on the two fortresses. There was no way the defenders could prevail in their desperate fight. The youngest of the Pulaski brothers, Anthony, fell earlier into Russian hands and was immediately sent to prison in Kazan on the Volga River. After a stubborn resistance, Frank and his men were forced to abandon Żwaniec and the survivors made their way across the Dniester River to Chocim. The battle at Holy Trinity Trenches only intensified and continued well into the night turned into a day illumined with fires. Some of the żwaniec survivors, including Frank Pulaski and Maurycy Beniowski, crossed the Zbrucz River and joined Casimir. Their joint effort temporarily broke down the Russian assault, although in the long run nothing could avert the helpless situation. The Russian continued sending new detachments and rained the defenders with bombs and grape shots. Suzdal grenadiers entered the battle to the sound of their drum corps like on a parade. With some 200 defenders left alive, Casimir somberly reflected that he was closer to the second alternative in the confederates' motto "to win or to die." What could some 200 confederates, or even 500 for that matter, achieve using six antiquated cannon? Farmers and craftsmen who joined them were armed even worse. Casimir was bustling around his cannons discharging a few more volleys when the Russians penetrated the fortress. The confederates defended every entrenchment and every building. In this scenery, lit by fires, death was a tangible reality. The Russians pushed the defenders on the headland. The confederates around Casimir, numbering at the time no more than 200, knew they were brought to bay but harbored no thought of surrender. Russian jägers repeatedly attacked yelling "Urrah!" Confronted by the desperate heroism, the Russians briefly stopped their attack in order to pull their artillery higher up. Then in a happy twist of fate a little boy appeared and showed the confederates a concealed and dangerous trail leading to the other side of the River Dniester. During the stormy night and in howling wind, Casimir and his 200 men, leading their horses, descended to safety. When the attacking Russians took the place, the headland was deserted. "Check dungeons, check passages! Get them! Handcuff them!" commanders shouted orders. Casimir Pulaski and his men had disappeared.

Casimir Pulaski was a tireless warrior. Accompanied by his fanatical youngsters, ready to die for the cause, he continued his "cat and dog" games, hurting the new troops dispatched from Russia to subdue the "Polish rebellion," as they termed the Polish fight to preserve independence.

Motivated by the love of freedom and faith, dedicated to defend the Fatherland, the troopers facing foreign invaders were, however, inadvertently embroiled in the private goals and ambitions of the magnates: the Potockis, Lubomirskis, Krasińskis, Radziwiłłs and others.

Casimir Pulaski was oblivious of political complexities and animosities within the Confederacy. His only goal was to fight the enemies of Poland and join everybody who did the same.

THE STRUGGLE CONTINUED

*W*ith no winter headquarters, Casimir Pulaski was ever on the move, crisscrossing the country on the way toward the Ruthenian Voivodeship to look for new centers of resistance flickering here and there and assailing and annoying Russian forces with continuous flighty attacks while on the move. For a while he joined forces with Prince Martin Lubomirski, who was a pupil of the former electoral king Stanisław Leszczyński in Luneville in France and a golden youth who lived a life of revelry in Paris. Then Lubomirski thought of pursuing a military career and served under Frederick the Great. Soon he escaped with his detachment and carried out ambushes and robberies. Captured by the Austrians, he spent seven years in prison. Three years after his release, he joined the Confederacy but his roguish reputation persisted and his unit was more troublesome than warriorlike. Soon, Casimir left the prince who was officially charged, not with the faults of his misspent youth, but current dealings. The news of his brother's arrival at Sambor spared him explanations.

The brothers met on May 13, 1769. It was not a joyful reunion since they were primarily discussing the circumstances of their father's demise. Joseph Pulaski had died in-mid April in a Turkish prison in Jassy and his death was attributed to the plague, but the sons kept wondering how he had died. They could not rule out the possibility that he might have been killed on the sly ("in the eastern manner," they would say) to settle his leadership conflict with Joachim Potocki and Michael Krasiński. Frank, the eldest son, received a call to come and bury his father. With the Russian troops stationed on the border, he was unable to re-cross the Dniester River with the body. Joseph Pulaski was buried in the steppe close to a barrow near the tract to Mohylew, with the prospect of transferring his ashes to Polish soil later.

Worse came to worse, when during further fighting Frank's detachment was reinforced with the support of 200 Tartars: "a wild and unmanageable bunch." The way they operated would lend some support to Joachim Potocki's charges of misconduct. Even after Joseph's death he circulated a proclamation warning not to join the Pulaskis who—the proclamation read—"pursued their own adventures and not the confederate cause." Were it not for their father's last letter and testament, this would have made the Pulaski brothers angry and revengeful. "If you wish to revenge my imprisonment," wrote the father,—"and perhaps even my death, you will succeed in that only when you surpass everybody else in your eagerness and devotion to the Fatherland and her destiny entrusted to you in this trying predicament."

Luckily, few paid heed to Joachim Potocki's malicious proclamation as he still clung to his snug job away from the war scene. Most patriotic Poles perceived the Pulaskis as indefatigable and steadfast confederates. When the Przemyśl Land gentry confederated at Sambor adopting a modified version of the Bar Confederacy declaration, they voted Frank Pulaski their Marshal. The Bill of Confederacy gave credit to the deceased Joseph Pulaski and called Casimir a "titan famed for his heroic exploits."

The confederates realized they needed a solid fortress for their headquarters. The city of Lwów, where the idea of confederation first emerged, seemed to be the perfect choice. On May 31, 1769, the Pulaski brothers arrived there with 3,000 troops. Bierzyński joined them soon with 1,500 men. Although the city of Lwów and the Royal Garrison were sympathetic to the confederates, the commander of the fortress, Colonel Felicjan Korytowski, stubbornly refused to yield the fortress to the Confederacy, quoting his loyalty oath. Negotiations failed. Storming of the city followed. The civil war began. Casimir attacked through the not-walled, trench-protected segment and would have prevailed when Korytowski, undoubtedly a brave defender and a figure of authority, appeared ahead of his dragoons. City mansions owned by royal sympathizers, supportive of the King's pro-Russian policy, were burned down. Fighting continued through the night without achieving the desired result. Paled by anger and bleeding, Pulaski could not understand how a good Pole, like Korytowski, could remain indifferent and hostile to the Confederacy. There was no time to lay siege since substantial Russian forces were approaching from Rawa Ruska under Colonel Sambor and from Janów under Johann von Drevitz. Those who would like to justify Korytowski for remaining loyal to the legally elected authorities may learn that he obeyed the King and let the Russians in. The Russians occupied the city for three years to release it only to Austria when the Republic of Poland was divided among three predatory neighbors.

Forced to withdraw, the Pulaski brothers, encouraged by Lithuanian emissaries, rallied the troops and devised a bold plan to march them to the Northern part of the Commonwealth. They led a select cavalry of 1,000 via Puławy and Rawa toward Brześć (Brest) and took the town by a surprise attack. At Brześć, they issued a proclamation, addressed not so much to the inhabitants as to the magnates, stating that any resistance would be treated as treason, with serious consequences. It proved, though, that no such a threat was necessary, for all people of ranking, influence and distinction flocked to join the Confederacy. The new confederates included Kajetan Sapieha, Jan Klemens Branicki, Michael Ogiński, Michael Pac and others.

During the Lithuanian campaign, the Pulaski brothers divided functions between themselves. Frank was to take care of "politics," organizing conventions, and Casimir was in charge of military action. Now, moving towards Pińsk, Słonim and Słuck, the Pulaskis kept on absorbing new detachments on the march. In Terespol, the militia joined the Confederacy. In Wołczyn, property of the Ponia-towskis, they sequestered cannons and a ton of powder. Joseph Bielak, commander of a cavalry regiment, composed of the Lithu-anian Tartars, joined the Confederacy at that time. The regular, trained troops began to transform the mass in-levy composed of untrained volunteers into better military shape.

The army under the Pulaskis had grown to 5,000 men. With that power they might soon have reached for Wilno and then perhaps even for Warsaw. However, news of the new centers of the Polish "rebellion" mobilized fresh Russian troops. Colonels Wachtmeister, Knorring, Shubbe and Drevitz were dispatched toward Lithuania. Colonel Ushakov was the first to reach the confederates under Pulaski. Convinced of his superiority, he neglected to reconnaissance and was neither sure of the terrain nor confederate numbers before engaging June 6 in battle at Kukiełki. The result was his complete surrender. Casimir Pulaski was later criticized for merely disarming Russian soldiers and letting them go free. But how could he handle a thousand prisoners? The goal of his campaign was to protect Confederate conventions. Some limited military action was to serve as a wake-up call for the nation to inspire faith in its own strength and power. Serious hostilities would start when Turkey was ready for serious action. This was the reasoning of the politicized command and Pulaski was a mere soldier following his directives.

Another large battle of the Lithuanian campaign was the one fought at Słonim, a beautiful city, made by Hetman Ogiński into one of the wonders of the Polish Republic. The battle took place on the night of July 11, 1769. With the region's gentry assembling for a convention, Casimir quartered his army close to the city in a spot protected by the creek, Szczara, quite wide at that point. Careless of his Russian soldiers' lives, Colonel Wachtmeister attacked frontally, along the dyke. When the Cossacks made across the river on one wing, Casimir Pulaski made his practice-perfect maneuver with a pretend cavalry attack and brought the enemy straight under the fire of his bush-masked artillery. The enemy panicked under the gunfire and was pursed by the Confederates' best cavalry under Captain Bielak. The enemy dropped their banners and left behind several hundreds of the dead and wounded.

Unfortunately, once more, internal intrigues and private ambitions within the Confederacy leadership made it impossible to take advantage of this victory. The Lithuanian magnates were surprised and perhaps even a little annoyed by Pulaski's success. Casimir managed to capture yet another Russian banner at Połonka but did not hinder Wachtmeister from joining Drevitz. The "bosses," Michael Krasiński and Joachim Potocki, warned again from Turkey not to trust the Pulaskis. Michael Pac was named the Marshal of the Great Duchy Confederacy and Joseph Sapieha its Head Commander. Casimir's bold plan to immediately march toward Wilno, the capital of the Lithuanian Great Duchy, was scrapped now when Wachtmeister and Drevitz joined forces and Casimir was stripped of commandership. Casimir had several other successful encounters with the Russians at Mysz, Dworzec and Nołczadia but the brothers decided that their Lithuanian period was over and a new goal was needed. With a handful of faithful companions they proceeded to Ostrołęka. In its environs they possessed several villages they had inherited from their mother who was born Marianna Zieliński.

They split with the Lithuanians at Rajgród and, through the virgin Augustów forests, through Grajewo and Szczuczyn, they headed to their familiar area, counting on help from among their relatives and friends from the local gentry.

CASIMIR' S MARSHALCY

*T*he Pulaski brothers' arrival in Ostrołęka, in early August, 1769, coincided, not without forethought, with the Łomża regional convention. It was an important convention, preceeded by four springtime district conventions and it brought together the nobles of the Łomża land. True, the original goals of the Bar Confederacy were deeply impressed on the minds of the honest folks of Łomża but it can be also safely assumed that the convention must have been prepared in advance by the Pulaskis' supporters. The convention recognized the glory-covered Pulaskis as the originators of the Bar movement. Their military leadership, recent victories in Lithuania, a display of Russian banners they had captured—all that made a big impression on the convening gentry. The position of Casimir Pulaski was raised and discussed. To regain proper recognition and acceptance for further activities for the sake of the Confederacy, Casimir needed an official position. Frank held the title of Marshal of Przemyśl. Casimir was lacking a similar position. After hot debates, the Act of Confederacy for the preservation of freedom, Catholic faith and the national law and order was promulgated. Taking under consideration Casimir's fame and merits, the assembled gentry unanimously elected Casimir Pulaski the Marshal of Łomża. Until now, the title was held by an old friend of the Pulaski family, Simon Suski, who gladly ceded it to Casimir.

The festive and well-attended celebration, comparable to that at Bar a year-and-a half earlier, included Mass and a patriotic sermon. The bishop of Łomża compared Casimir to the Epominodas of Thebe and Fabius of Rome. After a military parade which followed, Casimir Pulaski took his oath of office, repeating after Jan Turno, Secretary of the Confederacy, the solemn oath "in the name of God Almighty" to devote his position and abilities to serve the Fatherland, defend freedom, law, order and the holy Roman Catholic faith until the final victory over the Republic's foes. Three representatives, Roch Klicki, Romuald Przyjemski and Simon Suski, were assigned for assistance to the newly elected Marshal of Łomża, and included at the forum of the Generality. Eighteen councilors were named to promote the Confederacy and raise funds. The Marshal of Łomża felt gratified that in the newly formed Command or Generality his voice would rank equal to a Potocki's or a Krasiński's. With a great deal of enthusiasm, a large sum of money, 140 thousand zlotys, was collected for the cause and handed to Casimir.

The brothers' Ostrołęka visit was shortened by the approach of Alexander Suvorov, the best colonel the Russians had and the future general in the fight against Napoleon.

A huge Turkish army stood at the Dnieper River ready to help those who would fight against Russia. This news prompted the Pulaskis to start marching in that direction returning to Bar, the place of origin. New hope enkindled, Confederacy attracted more and more followers. Jakub Zamoyski, Ordynat or 'heir in tail,' was willing to bestow his Zamość fortress on the confederates under the condition that they would guarantee him a secure passage to Hungary or Silesia. This could imply that at the time the Russo-oriented Familia was changing their attitude and drifting closer to the Confederacy.

Unfortunately, negotiations to make Zamość their "place d' armes" failed and the Pulaskis, supported by youth with knightly hearts, turned back to their original plan of proceeding southeast toward Brześć and Kobryń. Alexander Suvorov pressed them on almost all sides. To make the situation worse, Wachtmeister's troops from Grodno stood across their way. The encircled brothers, trying to retreat toward Włodawa, got into a trap. The marshy terrain favored the enemy.

The Russians attacked unexpectedly and swiftly, and seriously threatened the defenders. A fierce battle lasted several hours. After the artillery was called to the rescue, the enemy was temporarily halted. This allowed the confederates time to make a hardship withdrawal, in rain and mud, to the west. Extremely exhausted, they crossed the River Bug and slowly proceeded eastward.

Unfortunately, there, too, the enemy was waiting for them. Trying to escape anywhere, the confederates reached the city of Włodawa. They had barely fallen asleep for less than one hour, they were awakened by an alarm. The enemy had entered the city. The confused confederates panicked. Casimir at the forefront of his brave units desperately resisted. His brother Frank rushed to help him. The furious fight on "cold weapons," meaning sabers and knives, continued.

The Russian soldiers, enticed by a big reward, chased the Pulaski brothers trying to take them alive. "Urra! Pulashchuk popal!" they shouted surrounding Casimir. When his horse fell, all seemed to be lost. In this tragic moment, Frank with a group of men appeared. Casimir jumped on another horse and was again in the middle of the action. He slashed the attackers until they withdrew. For a brief moment, the Russians under Colonel Rönne seemed to have been repulsed. The bleeding Casimir had barely time to breathe or realize what had happened when another column of Russian troops, led by Castelli, approached and tried to make a formation for shooting. Desperate Frank ran directly at Castelli, who right at that moment fired his pistol from a distance of a few yards, killing Frank Pulaski on the spot.

Meanwhile, more and more of Suvorov's fresh units poured in. Barely alive, wounded in the arm, Casimir with the small remainder of his soldiers, protected by a heavy rain, had withdrawn to safety. Later on, he found out that his brave brother Frank had been buried in Włodawa in a common grave by the Paulite monks.

Even though, in Suvorov's reports to St. Petersburg, the "Polish rebellion" was extinguished, the confederates continued their freedom fighting against the overpowering Russians.

GENERALITY

*S*everal days after the Włodawa defeat, wounded and feverish, Casimir Pulaski was back in action, organizing fresh troops. As early as September 20, 1769, he arrived at the confederate camp at Grab with 300 men and took part in a rally of his personal "opposition party" at the nearby Zborowo. Bishop Adam Krasiński, Prince Radziwiłł, Ordynat Jakub Zamoyski, Ignacy Bohusz, Teodor Wessel and several important Potockis, and Ossolińskis, were all there.

The formal occasion for this rally was the wedding of Marianna Ossolińska and Joseph Mniszech. However, on such occasions, important Confederacy matters were discussed. At this wedding, regardless of existing friction, important questions were brought up and debated, and amid toasts and dances decisions concerning appointments were reached.

The Marshal of Łomża was not favored by some of powerful figures like Bishop Adam Krasiński, the wise man of the Confederacy, Ignacy Bohusz, its most energetic proponent, and Lady Anna Jabłonowska, prime among women active in politics. Fortunately, however, some magnates like Paul Michael Mostowski, Mazovian Voivode, and a few others were on his side and supported Casimir's bold ideas.

Soon after, on October 31, the party gathered again at Biała in Cieszyn Silesia where Bishop Adam Krasiński brought to conclusion the long brewing idea of establishing a General Council of Confederated Estates, for short Generality. After all the difficulties, the idea finally took shape at that gathering thanks to the Bishop's political prowess. He managed to persuade all to adopt his way of thinking to "preserve and continue what was the best in the Bar Confederacy." Michael Krasiński and Joachim Potocki, still away in Turkey, were both kept as, respectively, the head of the civilian

Confederacy for Poland proper and the Commander-in-Chief of the Generality. Until the time of their return, a temporary command was put into the hands of a few other magnates, namely Michael Pac, Joseph Sapieha, who was, in general, judged to be inept, and Ignacy (Ignatius) Bohusz, secretary.

Marshal Casimir Pulaski could not approve such an arrangement and, for the time being, decided to stay apart even though his title enabled him and obligated to participating in the works of Generality. In spite of Princess Francesca's effort to draw him closer to her uncle, Bishop Adam Krasiński, he followed his own plan. He withdrew into the Carpathian Mountains and spent there the fall and early winter recruiting and training confederate soldiers.

With the failure to draw out the Turks (they withdrew to Moldova soon after their first attempt to battle the Russians), the absentee commanders still lingering on at Varna, the Generality assumed full control and attempted to draw Prince Karol Wettin of Dresden to head the confederated armies.

In this hiatus, some differences in evaluating the situation between Casimir Pulaski and the Generality surfaced. Pulaski continued to keep his own company and dispatched arrogant replies to letters sent him by Michael Pac on the behalf of Generality. The Generality suspected his dedication. Although the Mostowski clan considered him to be one of theirs, rumors were replete. Some remembered his old liaison with the robber-prince Lubomirski. In Warsaw, he was also rumored to be close to being won over by the King. A Saxon spy had an eye on him and may have harbored some calculations. "He harbors some wild grudges," reported Pac to Bishop Krasiński. In general, he was viewed as a positive, if—to put it bluntly—a difficult person to deal with. His stubborn streak, independent judgment and biting wit offended and worried Francesca. Many people claimed to having a role in making him step into line and approve Generality. But Francesca was most likely the one to affect his decision, when finally, on December 10, 1769, he brushed aside his resentments and objections, and signed an official "Jurament" and accepted the authority of the Generality. Casimir censured leadership and was heard to remark that from among all the Confederacy marshals he was the one who did "most fighting and least voting."

However, the creation of the Generality as a central command for the Confederacy, meant the country, unified under one leadership, could present a single face and voice to Europe. This also affected the royal camp, especially the Familia. Represented by Czartoryski uncles, the Familia camp was trying to rebuild its reputation, and joined voices to demand the ousting of the Russian troops from the Polish territory. They attempted to reconcile with the Confederacy. Ambassador Repnin was forced to hand in his resignation since he could not control the situation and safeguard the Russian interests. The King himself showed some signs of integrity in dealing with the Russian Empress.

The mission of reconciling with the Bar movement in order to build, with the support of France, a unified front against Russia was undertaken on behalf of the Familia by Grand Marshal Stanisław Lubomirski and former Chancellor Zamoyski. Bishop Ignacy Krasicki headed the Confederate delegation to Paris. Familia politicians, especially the King and his "talebearers," were not consistent. Casimir Pulaski professed that further success of the Confederates depended on their striking power, the positive attitude of the entire nation, and a firm belief in victory.

He understood better than anyone that the Poles would not be able to defeat the Russians in regular battles, especially when the Russians used their well-trained and battle-scarred foot soldiers. The only reasonable way of conducting warfare was his partisan tactics. Even when surrounded on all sides he was able to retreat. He never shunned from action when he could inflict losses on the enemy. His political program was to awaken and bestir the entire nation. Casimir set an example and called the nation to organize and his call was heard all over the Republic. The gentry flocked to the army. He was in particular responsible for influencing the Ruthenia, Przemyśl, Lublin, Brześć, Chełm, Volkovysk, Grodno, Wilno, Podolye and Łomża areas.

Casimir had no equal in popularity except for Sawa Czalenko (Calinski) who was a Cossack or Ukrainian peasant, and a non-commissioned officer in the Prussian army before joining the Confederacy. Both men had heard about each other, but they only met in Biała, at the signing of the pledge of loyalty to Generality at the close of 1769.

Now more and more volunteers poured into Casimir' camp in Grab. Despite shortages in supply, he attempted to have them uniformly dressed. All the cavalry wore the same navy-blue uniforms with red trousers and four-corner caps, "rogatywki." The Infantry wore off-white jackets and red trousers, conforming to Polish national colors.

Casimir greeted the year of 1770 in the field, not at an aristocratic ball in the safe refuge behind the Austrian border. He headed a cavalry raid against Russian forays at Sędziszów. In January, the Russians attacked the camp at Grab in full force. During the fierce three-hour battle Casimir, wounded in the right arm, bravely defended his camp and defeated the attackers.

This event opened the eyes of confederate leaders, headquartered in Prešov, and they decided to pay tribute to Casimir Pulaski. On January 26, 1770, a vindication act was issued stating that the Marshal of Łomża, beyond all suspicions, showed true patriotism and bravery, with no private end in view, and had documented this with his own blood. In consideration, thereof, the Generality held void and condemned all previous writings, manifestoes, and bills defaming the Pulaskis.

In February the Generality started paying regular soldier's pay.

On his way to Prešov, Casimir had to face again, at Gorlice, the crushing superiority of the Russian force under Commander Yelchaninov coming from Lwów. Loss of life in that bitter battle included the brave Marshal of Warsaw Tressenberg and his aide-de-camp Golion and some 200 confederate soldiers. Casimir was spared, though his detachment was badly decimated.

In June 1770, Casimir was at the seat of Generality in Prešov when Kaiser Joseph II paid a semi-official visit. At a grand ball, attended also by Princess Francesca, people whispered between themselves about Casimir's conversation with the Kaiser. With his distinguished appearance and refined manners, the Marshal of Łomża cut a stylish figure. Incredulously, for the prior two years,

50

this man had spent his days on horseback in marches, skirmishes and bloody fights.

At one moment an Austrian aide-de-camp in a white uniform, bowed before Casimir, "Ich habe die Ehre Ihnen bekannt zu machen, dass Seiner Majestaet bitten Sie, Herr von Pulaski" (I have the honor to report that His Highness invites you Sir, Count Pulaski).

Followed by the eyes of all guests, with guards presenting swords, Casimir was led to the "Roman Caesar" of the German nation, the King of Hungary and Czechs. Joseph II sat in a golden chair, in the company of his generals.

Greeting Casimir, he said: "Your greatness is known in foreign lands. Did you serve in foreign armies, maybe under the King of Prussia? Where did you learn the military trade so well?"

Pulaski mentioned his service for Karol Wettin of Saxony, but above all he stressed the importance of daily practice.

"Whom are you counting on?" asked the Monarch, curious what countries Casimir would mention.

"We have the righteousness of our cause on our side," Pulaski retorted. "We have the blessing of the RomanCatholic Holy See. Also, we have the good will of the people who back the war against Russia."

"It hardly seems sufficient,"said the Monarch. "You need allies who would profit from it."

Casimir Pulaski retorted that Poland was not the only country threatened by the growing powers of Russia and Prussia–Prussia had recently annexed Silesia. "The hospitality granted us by Austria ought to bring our countries closer..." he continued.

Casimir talked about the international situation to the emperor's dislike. A representative of enlightened absolutism, Joseph II was more interested in opposing the Catholic Church than the growing Russian-Prussian threat. Casimir was stunned to witness a new turn of the policy in action.

At that time, most of the fighting with the Russians took place near the Polish-Austrian border. According to a silent agreement, the Poles would take refuge beyond the border, if necessary. Some time, in August 1770, two Russian divisions, headed by Drevitz and Shakhovskoi, attacked Pulaski. He was driven across the Austrian border into the Austrian territory. Casimir counted that General Esterhazy, whom he knew personally from that encounter with the Kaiser's staff, would check the Russian pursuit. To his great surprise, the confederates were fired upon from the Austrian side. A desperate counterattack followed, aimed at saving the infantry and several light cannons. They succeeded but the confederate cavalry suffered big losses.

At one time a repugnant Prussian mercenary in the Russian service, Commander Drewicz vel Drevitz, wished to meet Pulaski personally to exchange opinions. When Casimir refused, fearing duplicity, Drevitz turned up, without an announcement or an invitation, at Casimir's headquarters at Cegiełka. A confederate guard brought two individuals to a village inn where Pulaski was stationed. One of them, short, husky and drunk, was Colonel Drevitz and the other, taller one, was Captain Vedenyapin. The obscure Drevitz tried to persuade Pulaski to leave the Confederacy and join the Russian empress' army. In his nonsense talk, he expounded on advantages of leaving senseless resistance to serve the Russian empress and he did not fail to stumble on his hatred toward the Poles (he found it offensive that his Prussian name sounded Polish to some). The irritated Casimir ordered them to leave and never come back because in the future they can only talk with weapons. "As intruders, you deserve to be arrested and executed. Letting you go free is a gesture of Polish chivalry," he said.

Another time, directly from the battlefield, reeking of sweat and smoke, Pulaski arrived at Zborowo where among those "not fighting, but voting" confederate leaders, he met for the first time Colonel Charles-François Dumouriez, head of the French mission. The immensely ambitious Dumouriez (he became France's minister of foreign affairs under the Revolution) followed the failed mission headed by Toulès and Chateaufort. Now, Dumouriez's activity was promising more concrete results. The Frenchman hastily reviewed the confederate army units and wondered how Russia had a problem

52

defeating those shabby, barefoot, poorly armed, and pious soldiers. "What kind of a country, what kind of people are you?" he asked and calculated what difference arms and provisions would make.

On his way to Poland, Dumouriez met with Prince Karol Wettin, who gave him first-hand information about Casimir. When Pulaski was introduced, he reluctantly said: "Ah, c'est vous ce celebre Pulaski, the bold one, who, as I hear, does not want to obey directives of the general plan." Casimir replied in his fluent French that had never heard about a general plan and that boldness was not a vice in war. "Of course," the Frenchman interrupted and added that what the confederates needed was more infantry and strongholds-fortresses, "comprenez vous?" (you understand?) Casimir Pulaski appreciated infantry and fortresses, but by his horseman's experiences, he knew it took years for infantry to be equipped with arms and trained. The training of cavalrymen and horses would not require as much, considering that the patriotic youngsters, who knew horseback riding, could jump on it right away. Therefore, in the present situation, Pulaski's viewpoint was more suitable and had been proved by his successes in the partisan warfare.

Casimir tried to persuade Dumouriez, but the colonel refused to be convinced, and for the Commander-in-Chief of the Generality he proposed the "yes man, "Joseph Miączyński. Casimir gave up further argument and following the Frenchman's directives, marched out into the field. He joined forces with his relative Michael Walewski. They sent the infantry back to Dumouriez for training and, on their horses, they fought the enemy wherever possible.

After discovering that the Russian Drevitz had left a small garrison in Cracow and was now heading toward Poznań, they decided to try their luck with a maneuver against the Russian-controlled Jagiellons' capital. First, they captured the outpost at Wawel Castle. Its Royal regiment surrendered and joined the Confederacy. Chances of winning were at hand. The Russians came from Cracow to the rescue of their Wawel outpost. Repelled, they barricaded themselves behind the city gates. The controversial decision of the confederate seniority was to not storm the city and risk Russian reprisal.

Casimir, who had his share of defending and taking fortresses, did not take the risk either.

Casimir returned to Skalbmierz where the news was waiting for him that Drevitz, greedy for the monastery treasures, was heading toward Częstochowa. Pulaski's idea was to get there first. Drevitz tried to block the way but at that time Pulaski had an upper hand and Drevitz withdrew in the direction of Warsaw. The confederates, numbering 2,500 men, under the command of Casimir Pulaski and Walewski, passed Miechów, and on September 8, 1770, reached the monastery of Częstochowa. However, the fortress famous for its defense during the Swedish invasion of Poland in 1655, or the so-called "Swedish Deluge," refused to admit the pious confederates within its walls.

DEFENSE OF CZĘSTOCHOWA

he Prior of the Paulite order did not chose to follow the
example of his famous predecessor, Father Augustyn
Kordecki, who during the "Swedish Deluge" of 1655
withstood the Swedish siege. His resistance altered the course of
events, leading to the Swedish defeat and expulsion. The current superior was terrified when he visited Pulaski at his camp at the monastery
gates. He tried to persuade him to steer away from the fortress. The
monks would not admit the army within the walls, but made an excep-
tion for the marshal himself, two officers and a chaplain.

The anniversary celebration at the Clara Mons or Bright Mount
marking the coronation of the Holy Virgin's miraculous painting
brought Nuncio Angelo Maria Durini to the monastery from Rome.
Casimir attended the Mass, then paid his respects to the Nuncio and
invited him to the confederate camp. The Nuncio visited that after-
noon, and blessed the confederates. Pulaski and Walewski took advantage of the visit, and, undoubtedly with his consent, escorted the
Nuncio's party back to the monastery, thus bringing the soldiers within its walls. The Paulite fathers did not stop worrying about the
Russian revenge and reprisals but found it easier to accept the accomplished fact after Pulaski had tricked them and moved the army inside
the fortress, relieving them of the responsibility for the decision.

For the confederates, taking Częstochowa was a breakthrough. It
kindled a new hope for success and influenced those who were still
hesitant whether to join the Confederacy. The fortress, which had
withstood the Swedish siege, was recently reinforced. It formed
a quadrangle, with on one side the two-spired church and with other
monastery buildings on the other three, strengthened by four octag-
onal towers. The quadrangle was surrounded by ramparts walled and
with casements and cannon at each corner. The entire fortress was
encircled by a moat with an inside stockade and had a marshy fore-

front. Casimir found the fortress well stocked with 140 cannon and a full supply of missiles. Pulaski undertook further improvements on fortifications, consulting French specialists, General de Labadie and Captain d'Etannion, in preparation for an inescapable assault.

While the work was progressing, Casimir Pulaski undertook a risky escapade to Lubliniec in Silesia, dictated by his heart, to visit Princess Francesca. They were both deeply moved but mainly talked of politics. She was trying to encourage him to cooperate with Joseph Zaremba, commander of the well-organized Great Poland (Poznań Voivodeship) confederates who were a formidable armed force. Casimir, who never refused Francesca's advice, met with Zaremba in early October. Jędrzej Kitowicz, the best memoirist of the period, reported that they spent three days together exercising and parading their soldiers before one another. Pulaski tried to talk Zaremba into joining forces to strike against Drevitz together. However, they both had equal rank under the Generality and neither one was willing to yield to the other. Shared command made no sense to Zaremba who decided to split "for the good of the cause," as he stated, to reduce the burden on the countryside.

Disappointed, Casimir left his infantry in Częstochowa, and with his faithful and brave cavalry unit resumed his partisan tactics, trying to confuse Russian generals and thwart their plans with his wide-ranging sorties taking him as far as Poznań. His clever maneuvering was evidence of his skill.

Meanwhile, on October 22, 1770, the Generality, instigated by France, passed a resolution deposing King Stanisław August Poniatowski. They declared an interregnum. Casimir, a man of action, received the news with the same reservation with which he had read other manifestoes filled with thundering words and of little substance. He definitely did not side with the agitators like Frank Kożuchowski, Simon Kossakowski and others who had solicited his support for the King's dethronement by appealing to common memories of their first clashes with the Russians in Mitawa or Repnin's misdeeds at the time of the Radom Confederation.

Hot-headed in battle as he was, he refrained from playing politics, and stayed away from the Generality's convoluted maneuvering and contradictory moves that animated that body. Foremost in his mind was the problem of defending Częstochowa from danger of assault and siege. At the end of November he intercepted an instruction to Drevitz from the Russian High Command, specifying how many extra men and weapons he would get to lay siege to Częstochowa. The letter further instructed that after the victory the monastery was to be occupied by the Russian army and defenders sent in stages to Siberia.

At the time the Generality's forces consisted of approximately 20,000 men, of which 3,000 were under Casimir Pulaski's command. With this force, he was incessantly dogging and harassing the Russians in the Częstochowa region, and outsmarting Colonel Drevitz with his forays.

The last day of 1770 was marked as the first day of the Russian assault against Częstochowa. On a cold, frosty morning, at 9 o'clock, from behind the hills looking in the direction of Kłobuck, the vangard column emerged and Russian troops began pouring in. Pulaski started, without hesitation, firing cannons to impede their progress, making it impossible for them to dig in. During several hours of intensive shelling, a large number of attackers were killed and wounded. By evening, to clear out the foreground, Casimir gave orders to burn the city ourskirts occupied now by the Russians.

On January 3, a heavy concerto of Russo-Prussian artillery guns lasted an entire day and reached its crescendo by night. The monastery walls withstood the assault without significant damage and the fortress suffered no casualties. Next day, Russian Colonel Drevitz sent his negotiators calling for surrender and promising everyone a safe return home.

Full of self-assurance and swagger, Pulaski sent his response: "Tell your Drevitz, if he wishes to survive, he be better advised to put down his weapons by the monastery walls. In exchange, he will get a free passage to St. Petersburg." Later, during the same night, despite heavy bombardment, ordered by the angry Drevitz, Casimir Pulaski and his soldiers made a daredevil attack from the Lubomirski gate. In darkness they attacked the enemy battery on three sides. To the Russians concentrating on loading and firing the guns, it came as a total surprise. They darted away, followed by an attack with all kinds of weapons, including hammers they had brought with them. By the time Drevitz managed to get the situation under control, the Poles rendered three of his largest cannons harmless and withdrew with few casualties. The defenders continued firing at the Russians who chased the sally within the firing range of the monastery walls. This happened on the Orthodox Christmas Eve and some Russian soldiers whispered among themselves about the miracle-working quality of this strange place.

Over the next several days Russian artillery bombarded hard without causing much damage. This forced Drevitz to contemplate storming the fortress. Preparations were visible all the morning. Russian soldiers were driving groups of miserable local peasants to cart fascines and ladders. On January 9, it looked like they were about to retreat. Pulaski was on alert when the assault started. On January 9 at 2 o'clock, three Russian columns emerged from the suburban ruins. The storm columns of Russians, dazed with vodka, pushed ahead bunches of unfortunate peasants carrying fascines and ladders. Watchful as ever, Casimir Pulaski ran along the Polish positions to halt an untimely response. The moats filled with attackers who raised ladders to the walls and began climbing. Then Pulaski responded. He lit up the battlefield with wreaths on fire and ordered the throwing of rocks, logs, fireballs, storm-pots and grenades to the accompaniment of firing guns, pistols, carbines and all other weapons available, hitting attackers rows after rows.

It took an hour or so for the assault to collapse. The defenders continued shooting at the withdrawing Russians troops for a few more hours. To compound the Russian defeat, they rushed out of the gates at daybreak to follow the withdrawing attackers and collect abandoned weapons, rifles, sabers, bayonets and ammunition. Next day it was quiet but one could observe preparations in the Russian camp for another assault against the Jasna Góra.

However, the Russians did not decide to attack. On January 16, 1771, they began withdrawing, probably, because some Polish troops commanded by Miączyński and Szyc beleaguered the Russian garrison in Cracow. To improve the morale of his troups, Drevitz took hostages from the nearby Novitiate of St. Barbara. A dozen or so seminarians were stripped to their underwear, and he ran them barefoot in the snow. Pulaski could not tolerate this and immediately charged forth. He was always gracious to his war prisoners, usually letting them go free. The furious Drevitz was forced to abandon the poor victims. Withdrawing in a hurry, he burned some three hundred wagons with provisions, and pulled out.

GLORY, BUT NO SUPREME COMMAND

n February 1, 1771, Casimir Pulaski received a congratulatory letter from the Generality signed by Commander Pac. He praised Casimir's significant contribution to the defense of the monastery in fancy language, praising his "contempt for danger, foresight in command, courage in execution, influence on the course of future events, and an all-embracing sensibility he exhibited during his courageous and glorious defense of Częstochowa."

The next day, February 2, was the Candlemas Thanksgiving Holiday. During this celebration, the most heroic defenders, with Casimir Pulaski at the front, were decorated with the Bar Confederacy Cross. The Mass was celebrated and the bishop delivered a reassuring patriotic sermon. "You fought for 'faith' and Mary, for the law and the Fatherland'," he said quoting an inscription on the confederacy cross and superimposed Mary's picture. "Mary is the conqueror of the enemy, the queen of our country and of the Polish eagle. Under the eagle's sign conquer our enemies and drive away foreign domination."

Pulaski's fame as the defender of Częstochowa spread all over Europe. French, German, English and Dutch newspapers wrote at length of his exploits. Special congratulations came from Jean-Jacques Rousseau, conveyed through a Generality envoy in France. He wrote, "The Confederation will save their expiring fatherland." Casimir's name was pronounced with patriotic adoration in contemporary poetry and songs, next to the famous names of Zawisza and Czarniecki.

On his next visit to Lubliniec, Princess Francesca played and sang him one of those ballads: "Here comes, here comes Drewicz/ with three hundred horses/After him, after him comes Pulaski/with thousand horses..."

"You heard that?" she asked after a pause: "Without your command, my heroic lord/something bad will happen to our army." Also the Generality praised "the most distinguished marshal" in their writs. A demand was growing to make him an overall commander of the confederated army.

That was, undoubtedly, the most glorious period of the Confederacy. Sawa-Calinski and others visited the monastery, and expressed their admiration for the brave defenders. Even the ever hesitant King Stanisław August Poniatowski, influenced by the Zamoyskis and Czartoryskis, began resisting the Russian pressure.

Repnin's successor, the new Russian ambassador Michael Volkonski, who replaced the bankrupt Repnin, tried to repeat the intrigue similar to that of the Radom Confederation and created a so-called "Patriotic Council," aimed at creating a diversion in the Bar camp and frighten the King's supporters. It soon turned into a fiasco. Discredited, Volkonski was replaced by Kaspar von Soldern.

During the following winter and spring months, the confederates secured many victories. Commander Suvorov, nicknamed the Russian wolf, was severely beaten at Lanckorona. He lost almost his entire officer corps. Another time, the confederates took as prisoners two Polish generals in Russian service, Jan and Michael Grabowskis. However, this optimistic picture was spoiled by drawbacks on the Turkish front, where the Russians took Chocim and Jassy and established a new front at the River Danube.

The "miracle of Częstochowa" did not become a turning point in the struggle for independence, in repetition of the Częstochowa miracle of King John Casimir during the resistance against the Swedish invaders. It is true that history does repeat itself, but those are never exact repetitions. Events may recur skewed, as mock events or tragic comic events.

On March 28, 1771 the Generality convened the War Council at Biała. The streets were swarming with marshals and commanders. Pulaski, Zieliński, Kossakowski, Miączyński, and Walewski were all there, hopeful and anxious for important decisions to take place. They were also critical and asked why the Generality ignored its commanders, did not trust them and stinted on funds. They inquired what the titular head commanders, Michael Krasiński and Joachim

Potocki, were doing abroad and were they planning to return only under the wing of a foreign army.

The Council awaited Colonel Charles-François de Périer Dumouriez' return from his diplomatic and provisions mission in France and Dresden. He returned on April 15 with only 22 cannon and limited ammunition and money. He was received reservedly, but when he presented his plan, the marshals, including Casimir Pulaski, expressed their approval. The plan called for holding Częstochowa, conquering Cracow and garrison fortresses. That was one thing. The other, equally important, was to fight east, to Podolya, at the back of the Russian army and, with the help the Turkish army, to give a crushing blow to Russia. France was to decisively go to war with Russia and to induce Sweden who had an old score against the Russian Tsarina, to do the same.

For the confederate forces to take a decisive and successful action required a commander who had universal authority. Most of the marshals considered Casimir Pulaski to be such a candidate and he himself was not adverse to the idea. He assumed that even if the Frenchman did not sympathize with him, he had no better candidate and would eventually propose him to the Generality as the head commander. However, the French advisor reserved the decision for himself. His opinion of Pulaski was as follows: "He is a young man, impetuous, more proud than ambitious," he wrote for the council, "a big enemy of the Potockis, extraordinarily brave and sincere in dealing with others, but very much undisciplined." He also left us a record of the numbers: "The army under his direct command consists of 600 hussars, 300 dragoons, 100 infantry, and close to 3,000 cavalry falling into seven squadrons. On top of that, he has under him 100 Tartars, 50 Bosnians and 40 Cossacks. Most marshals report to him, but mainly for the reason they do not want to obey orders."

Before long more and more discrepancies and conflicts arose between Pulaski and Dumouriez. Casimir did not disagree when the Frenchman commanded bonfires be lit on each hill in the area every night, solely to emphasize the power of the confederates. But when Dumouriez requested taking horses across the border to Hungary to sell them in order to convert most of the cavalry into infantry, Casimir was strongly opposed. He argued that one needed several years to train infantry and there was no time for that.

The two violently clashed at Skawina near Cracow. Trying to show superiority of the French rigor over Polish anarchy, Dumouriez courtmartialed three confederated soldiers for violence against the civilian population. The execution was to take place in front of the offensive confederate troops, not accustomed to such practices. It was just about to begin when Pulaski arrived and halted it. He demanded the death penalty be commuted into hard labor. Despite these conflicts between Dumouriez and Pulaski, Casimir considered their relations to be good. He was still counting on supreme command with his goal of initiating the general offensive.

On May 2, Casimir Pulaski left Biała leading 500 soldiers with 30 cannon toward Częstochowa. He carried belated soldiers' pay and Dumouriez' letter to Joseph Zaremba calling him to cooperate with Pulaski. In mid-May Casimir informed Dumouriez of his movement toward Siewierz. On the 19th of May he was at Zator. The next day the War Council decided to move him against the weakened frontier guards set up by Suvorov and Shakhovskoi in the Lublin area. Three days later, Colonel Dumouriez met with overwhelming Russian forces at Lanckorona and lost the battle. Then, to explain himself, he blamed the Poles baselessly and arrogantly though he had many words of praise for Casimir.

ZAMOŚĆ AND BACK IN CZĘSTOCHOWA

n May 25th, Casimir Pulaski beat the enemy at Dębica. Before reaching Majdan Kolbuszowski he defeated Colonel Polivanov's detachments and skillfully outmaneuvered Suvorov's main army. Then he crossed the River San and pushed on toward Zamość. En route, he dispatched a letter to the War Council and reported that he hoped his march was not "in vain." Pulaski advised his correspondents, "not to be taken in by human frailty which usually prevails" He considered Zamość a key to the control of the situation because of its proximity to the Turks who needed, he wrote, "an encouragement and our succor."

Leaving his infantry at strategic points on the way, he approached Zamość ahead of 2,500 cavalry. The city was aware of his movements and a delegation was sent to meet the confederates. Four city officials traveled in a carriage to meet the famous marshal. The city officers were Dzierżanowski, Wyszyński, Zakrzewski and Lipski. Casimir Pulaski was accompanied by two marshals, Philip Radzimiński and Tadeusz Przyłuski, when he met them. These negotiators quickly became persuaded by the marshals to join the Confederacy. The problem was convincing the garrison that had been recently sworn into neutrality. According to the city officials, most officers would not be in a hurry to give up their comfortable neutrality. A bold decision was made on the spot.

"I would be able to convince them if only I had a chance," declared Pulaski. They decided between themselves that three city delegates would stay and Pulaski and his marshals would enter the fortress in their carriage. The ploy worked and Pulaski drove straight to the headquarters to greet the astounded commander of the Zamość fortress, General Kwaśniewski.

"General," said Councilman Michael Dzierżanowski, "I present you Casimir Pulaski, Marshal of Łomża in general charge, a Hector of the Polish cause, with laurels of Bar, Berdyczów and Częstochowa, and his company: the Honorable Marshal Przyłuski of Czernihów and the Honorable Radzimiński, Marshal of the Sanok Land." "Outside these walls, several thousands of our troops are encamped," added Pulaski.

"What then are your intentions?" asked the Commander, uneasy and surprised.

"The interest of our Fatherland requires us to mutual action. General, you are invited to join with your forces. The City Commissioners have already sworn to the Confederacy, and we are only waiting to hear from you."

General Kwaśniewski quoted their privilage of neutrality, and expounded on their fears in the face of the overwhelming Russian superiority but, finally, became persuaded. He and Major Dobrzeński, his second in command, were sworn by Pulaski.

So far so good. All seemed to work well. Zamość would become another Częstochowa in the confederates' hands. The fortress would wear Suvorov's powerful army out trying to take it from the confederates, as did Częstochowa under siege by Drevitz. However, a mutiny broke out in the city. Lieutenant Jan Kober came to see Commander Kwaśniewski with several discontented officers and reported,

"Yours is a lost cause. There is nothing to be gained. We won't give the city up for destruction. We have sworn neutrality and who will release us from that oath?"

"You forget your rank, Lieutenant," said Pulaski. "It is up to your Commander to give orders and I am representing the Generality and the people of Poland whose will is to throw off the yoke of captivity. You propose to outstay the events at the comfort of a chimney corner?"

"Nobody can win against the mighty empress. Bloodshed would just be useless," said another officer.

"We are paid soldiers' pay to serve the king, and will not support troublemakers."

General Kwaśniewski remained quiet and Pulaski was outraged, "Who is the Commander here? What sort of officers are those allowed to debate during wartime? Call guards and put them in the stocks."

The officers withdrew, but they did not resign from the opposition. Lieutenant Kober called the officers for a briefing. The majority voted Commander Kwaśniewski guilty of perjury and ousted him from his position. A new commander was elected who appeared before Pulaski to order that the confederates leave the fortress. Pulaski did not give up easily. He still trusted that his name would work miracles and still hoped that he might somehow influence the soldiers of the garrison and the townspeople.

He persuaded the new commander to give him some time and still tried to win Zamość for the confederates. Pulaski prevailed on Bishop Anthony Okęcki of Chełm to make use of sacerdotal powers vested in his office to release the officers from their neutrality oath. That made no difference. Pulaski and his marshals considered all means and ways to keep the fortress.

The neutrality supporters did not loose time either. They spread rumors among the townspeople of an immense army a day's march away from the city. That piece of news filled the city with anxiety and discontent. Pulaski had to take under consideration that were he to defend the city under siege, he could not count on their loyalty and would have to beware of betrayal.

"No chance for another Częstochowa," was Pulaski's bitter remark. "We have to leave."

Suvorov who had the tzarina's special orders to capture Pulaski boasted that this time "Pulaszczuk" would not escape his pursuit. He made hundreds of miles daily, devised ambushes and stake-outs, fought several skirmishes every day. Hard as he tried, his goal kept escaping him. To make it easier on himself and justify his failure, Suvorov called Casimir's retreat from Zamość a "masterful escape" and sent him a china fox as a sign of his congratulations. He followed Pulaski to Tarnów, then gave up his pursuit.

Pulaski arrived safely in Częstochowa on the 18th of June. Soon afterwards Casimir visited Princess Francesca in Lubliniec who kept worrying and inquiring about him in her letters to her uncle, Bishop

Krasiński. It was in Lubliniec that Casimir found out about the terrible defeat of the confederates under Colonel Dumouriez's command at Lanckorona. Angry for his defeat and humiliated, Commander Dumouriez blamed Poles for his overthrow, and threatened to cut short France's support for the confederates.

In late June, Drevitz again besieged the monastery of Częstochowa. This time he was assisted by the Royal Army, commanded by Ksavery Branicki, the one who married Empress Catherine's natural daughter. The attackers did not feel secure with Joseph Zaremba gathering numerous confederated regiments at their back, behind the Kłobuck Forest.

Despite failed earlier attempts to arrive at an understanding, Pulaski continued to strive for Zaremba's cooperation. Zaremba consulted with him in Częstochowa but was unwilling to commit himself. Undecided, he promised to think it over and be back in three days but was heard remarking at the gate: "I will never set foot here again."

One day, during artillery fire exchanged from both sides, the enemy's parliamentarian arrived reporting that his Highness, Master of the Royal Hunt Commander Ksavery Branicki wished to confer with Pulaski. Casimir was not prone granting such talks, but out of curiosity, agreed to see him to learn what the King—Royal Traitor—wished to offer. Pulaski met Branicki in the company of Drevitz, amidst the roaring of the cannons. Casimir became indignant and refused to discuss anything in the company of the bandit and that noise.

"I did not come here to attack you but to offer our concord and friendship," said Branicki.

"In that the company you keep?" retorted Pulaski.

They both agreed to arrange for the next day's meeting with no witnesses present. The central idea behind the proposed talks was to bring about the reconciliation between the king and the confederates. Branicki called for surrendering the fortress and preached on the country's misfortunes and the evils of the civil war. Pulaski did not rule out reconciliation on condition that the king's party would join in demanding the removal of all Russian armies from Poland.

Disappointed, Branicki left with angry words, "You will be sorry you missed the opportunity." These were the very words Pulaski had heard from the drunken Drevitz who had paid him an unexpected visit in his camp at Cegielka. Branicki made a note in his diary: "He [Pulaski] spoke as a young bighead." Again, Drevitz and Branicki who accompanied Drevitz, had to abandon the siege and withdraw from Częstochowa.

On July 15, 1771, the Generality officially named Casimir Pulaski the Commander of the Częstochowa fortress, and that raised his position and esteem, as he was now one of the three top commanders of the Confederacy, with the prerogatives to make decisions regarding war tactics and strategies.

With Colonel Dumouriez about to leave his post, Princess Francesca made an attempt to have them reconciled. They met at Łojki and Casimir gave his report on the number of soldiers under his command. He declared his intent to keep discipline among his regimental officers and soldiers and to dismiss unsuitable persons. He also agreed not to undertake any action without advising the War Council–a mere formality since he himsef was a member of the Council, and was granted authority to nominate the two others. The Frenchman, on his part, made it clear that it never was his intent to assume direct command, and reminded Pulaski that his decisions were always co-signed by the War Council. He admitted he had no right to impose warfare methods for which no conditions existed. He promised not to interfere any longer. It was generally known that Dumouriez was leaving to be replaced by a new advisor from France, General Anthony Charles Vioménil. The reconciliation at Łojki was aimed at improving the atmosphere in the Confederates' army and highlighting Pulaski's rank. As Commander of the Częstochowa fortress, Pulaski reached the top position.

Pursuant to the Generality's order, Casimir Pulaski left Częstochowa. With his cavalry, infantry and artillery, he crossed the Vistula River at Bobrójsk and on the 25th of August he reached Tyniec. He learned of Zaremba's victory over Branicki. Casimir sent a letter to congratulate him the victory and remarked that "they both were penalized because of their mutual indifference" and now God grant them another opportunity to act together to successfully defeat the enemy of the Fatherland.

Endeavoring to reorganize the confederated army, Casimir proposed to appoint five general commanders and to take Warsaw. He judged this could be achieved with an army of 50,000 men. He headed a well-trained army of 6,000. With the arming of the Kurpie free men he expected to grow to 8,000. The new French advisor, General Vioménil, supported Pulaski's plan of conquering Warsaw by using the two largest corps, Zaremba's and Pulaski's, under their dual command. At that time, Casimir's popularity, eagerness and optimism disturbed many important people here and abroad, as Anna Jabłonowska wrote in 1771 from Rotterdam. The adherents of Russian rule in Poland and Poland's enemies raked their brains to find a ruse to ruin Pulaski and bring him down.

DIRTY TRICK

*S*tanisław Strawiński was first heard of when at the close of 1770 he attended the King's audience in the Warsaw Castle, and asked the King for a donation on account of his difficult situation. He received 10 ducats in gold. Some time later, at another audience, he handed the King his plea in writing which, when unfolded at night, turned out tó be the Generality's manifesto declaring a vacancy on the Polish throne.

At that time, the Confederacy had not yet developed a uniform position on dethronement and definitely was far from having the idea broadcast. The King was shown the manifesto that night. He ordered his men to locate the one who had the nerve to serve it and bring him in for further inquiries. The person could not be found in Warsaw because, as we know now, he was gone to take his all-important mission to Casimir Pulaski.

Strawiński arrived in Częstochowa at the close of July, 1771, and when he was finally admitted to see Pulaski his story was that he had joined the Confederation two years ago. He had no pressing need for money, having sold his village in Lithuania but what he had, his funds and his reputation included, he was willing to sacrifice to destroy the impostor on the throne. According to Strawiński's own deposition, taken later on, Casimir rebuked him, and said that the King's death would not accomplish anything because the Confederacy was not powerful enough to dispose of the Polish throne. In the course of further conversation, Pulaski allegedly agreed that Strawiński would kidnap the King and bring him to Częstochowa.

Pulaski actually met Strawiński once, or perhaps even twice, and in the near future would pay dearly for his mishandling of the matter. First, he should have had the guy expressing this gruesome initiative arrested and checked. Strawiński's claim that he acted on his own, being unable as a confederate to look idly at the Russian puppet on the Polish throne, required thorough investigation.

Who was he? Was he a maniac or a madman or perhaps an agent provocateur? Alas, constantly busy, Pulaski did not have time to do the checking but the idea probably crossed his mind when he, allegedly, re-invited the visitor "to come back in a fortnight."

According to Strawiński's testimony the second meeting took place on August 15, 1771. In general, Pulaski's biographers accepted that during that meeting, Casimir Pulaski gave no instructions and took a position against the regicide but, supposedly, he agreed to the kidnapping of the monarch. Strawiński's suspicious reputation was never checked. This could have been attributed to naivete and recklessness on the part of Pulaski but the fact was that it was virtually impossible to gather credible information in the hubbub of confederate battles and forays.

Too much credit has been given to Strawiński's claim that he acted on his own. That much seems obvious. The alternative seems to have never been given equal consideration. The Latin proverb has it, "Id facit qui prodest." It is done by who profits. The profiter is the doer.

Who could have profited from it? With our hindsight knowledge, we know who could have been interested in compromising the acclaimed hero and leader of the anti-Russian confederacy. Almost certainly, it was not Strawiński's private business, but cunning Russian diplomacy that stood behind him.

Some commentators, basing again on Strawiński's deposition, never contested his statement that it was Pulaski who lent a hand to help the coup d'état and borrowed 26 men from Łukawski's detachment. How could this have been possible when Łukawski was not under Pulaski's command? Also, it is known from other official sources that the alleged assassins were recruited by a Cossack named Kuźma-Kosiński, another person initiated into the secret mission, who–like Strawiński–was never called to account for his part. On the contrary, he was rewarded, and later resettled in Italy for a quiet and modest life. As to the group of 26, they need not have known, and most likely did not, what was really going on.

Pulaski was not likely to remember the obscure Strawiński during the busy months of September and October of 1771. Constantly busy and on the go, he was making new plans that would bring hope for the country. At that time, actions against the Russians picked up considerably. Michael Ogiński from Lithuania, well-known composer of polonaise music and author as well as the builder of the canal, proved to be an equally talented commander. He led the victorious battle at Bezdzież in which the Russian commander, Colonel Albichev, lost his life and over 1,000 of his troops were killed, missing in action or taken prisoner.

Pulaski persistently hoped that Princess Francesca would find a way to convince the stubborn Zaremba about the necessity of joining forces with him. The heads of the Generality, including Pulaski, assembled in Zwierzyniec near Częstochowa to facilitate a Pulaski-Zaremba alliance. Casimir was pleased that Zaremba decided to appear in person. That, of course, made all the others happy as well, especially when Zaremba accepted the plans presented to him.

From October 2 to 13, Pulaski and Zaremba, together with the help of French experts, worked out detailed plans to lay siege to Warsaw. Precise coordination of the two armies, Pulaski's and Zaremba's, was set up to the exactness of one day. The victorious commander Ogiński joined them in the march on Warsaw. On such a special occasion as this, before going into the battle, a grand ball was arranged for relaxation and a good mood.

"Some might have had fun with beautiful eyes," reported a participant. "Myself I was dazzled to see the Royal Princess who won Pulaski's complete confidence to facilitate our unanimity."

On October 20, Casimir Pulaski gathered his troops near Częstochowa and after receiving blessings from Bishop Adam Krasiński accompanied by his charming niece Francesca, started moving toward the capital. He proceeded according to the set plan, via Gilda, Przedbórz, Opoczno and Wielka Wola. After a few days, Casimir found out that Zaremba had failed again and that Russian Colonel Lange was marching against him with twice as many troops.

In that situation, Pulaski should have turned back to Częstochowa in order to save his army behind the fortress walls.

However, Casimir was not sure what was holding Zaremba back. Maybe he was just a little late. Then it would be not fair to leave him alone facing overwhelming Russian forces under Colonel Lange. In such distress, Pulaski waited two more days and then began withdrawal. But, it was a little too late.

Casimir presumed that Colonel Lang, in hot pursuit, would separate his cavalry from his infantry. Then, in that way, he would fall in a trap that had been prepared for him on the road to Iłża. Pulaski hid a portion of his cavalry behind the swamps with orders to charge the enemy from the rear. Colonel Lang attacked first the army service columns and Pulaski counterattacked with all his forces breaking down the fierce Cossack units. At that very moment, confederates from behind the swamps were supposed to attack from the rear. But to everyone's total astonishment, it did not happen. The confederates' detachment could not find its way to the battlefield, and simply got lost.

This battle, the most carefully and precisely planned of any of Pulaski's battles, ended with a total defeat. Pulaski himself could have been killed if one of his men, Grodecki, had not given him his horse. The vanquished Casimir Pulaski brought the rest of his troops to Częstochowa, and right away dropped by in Lubliniec to see Francesca. From there, he went to Cieszyn and Prešov, in order to report to the Generality's Command what had happened.

To his greatest astonishment, nobody was interested to listen or intended to investigate why Zaremba failed to keep up his part in the march against Warsaw. All they were talking about was the failed kidnapping of the king and that the assassins had acted on Pulaski's order.

"I did not have anything to do with that!" exclaimed Casimir, trying to assure them that it was all slander, and a nasty, vulgar lie.

THE KING KIDNAPPED

*O*n the dark and foggy night of November 3, 1771, a king's carriage carried Stanisław August Poniatowski through the streets of Warsaw. Returning from a visit to his ailing uncle, Michael Czartoryski, he was on his way to the castle. In Miodowa Street, a group of 26 "confederates," led by John Kuźma and Walenty Łukawski, attacked the king's carriage. The first shot killed a king's servant named Butzau, whose extremely beautiful wife was known to be later one of the King's well-paid mistresses (Could this be a clue that he was in on the plot?). Another servant, Mikulski, was wounded with a saber. The king himself took advantage of the chaos, and escaped from the carriage and headed to the gate of the nearby palace of his uncle.

A report published in Warsaw's "Monitor," dated November 27, 1771, elaborated: "During the brutish and quite savage abuse, one of the malefactors (Kuźma) aimed straight at the King's head and fired his pistol, but even at that time Providence protected His Majesty to the extent that during all that shooting the King felt only a hot spot on the side of his head where the bullet whizzed by.

"Ceasing to shoot whether because they had no pistols loaded or time to load them or for some other reason, they started to shower blows on the Monarch with their sabers, but the fur coat that clothed him protected him from other body damage except for bruises .... Only once was the King hit in the back of his head with enough force to leave a visible wound. In the meantime, to speed up their escape the malefactors forced the King, now without hat and with only one shoe, to get on a horse and ride with them .... They approached the city walls and were moving across the moat ... with the King forced to move along ... when the King's horse fell down beneath him once and then again, breaking its leg. In darkness of night and afraid that they would be overtaken, the offenders became disoriented, and could not figure out where they were supposed to go. Becoming agitated and fearful, they dispersed in all directions...."

Only one, Kuźma, "by a strange coincidence," remained with the monarch and brought him to the mill at Marymont. There, Kuźma, the one who had fired the shot at the king, was moved by the king's appeal and begged for forgiveness and pardon. The lucky king got a good night's sleep in the comfortable bed of a miller's daughter while a rustic was dispatched with the king's letter to the castle bearing the good news. The king was 'saved'."

At first, the king tried to make light of the incident, but later, influenced by people associated with the Russian empress, he would make a big issue out of the kidnapping. He would indulge occasionally in playing the martyr and hero who had escaped death.

All this suited the Russian empress very much. She just began negotiating with the courts of Prussia and Austria regarding the partitioning of Poland and received the new and strong argument she needed. This "provocation" turned out to be a more effective weapon in the tsarina's hands than all the corps of the Russian army together.

All the courts of the neighboring countries declared alliance with the Polish king. The French King Louis XV, who otherwise would have received willingly the news of the removal of Stanisław August Poniatowski from the Polish throne, revoked the promises he had made to the confederates because of the scandal.

Without any investigation, the perpetrators were declared to have acted on orders from Casimir Pulaski who became the principal target of accusations. On November 30, the Austrian authorities issued an order for Pulaski's arrest on the grounds of an attempted regicide.

A few days later, on December 4, the Generality, in order to save the Confederacy, decided to sacrifice Pulaski. Princess Francesca became indignant at human vileness, but even she cooled toward Casimir. She did not exclude the possibility of his inadvertent involvement in the affair of the king's kidnapping.

Domestic press here and all press abroad blew up the event, accusing Pulaski of all the fanciful atrocities he would do after lay-ing his hands on the monarch. All turned their backs on Pulaski, even those who before had cherished his friendship. What fortitude it took for Casimir not to break down! He returned to Częstochowa to start preparations for the fifth anniversary of the Confederacy. He elaborated new military offensives and, believing in his star, hoped that all was not yet lost.

Pulaski began writing letters to influential friends, trying to explain his situation and assure them regarding his innocence. First, Casimir wrote to the minister of France, Prince D'Aiguillon, explaining that the accusations of his participation in the attempt on the king's life, was an "abominable calumny without any grounds." D'Aiguillon informed General Vioménil and asserted his belief in Pulaski's innocence. Along with D'Aiguillon, the French General Vioménil thought that Casimir was not guilty and could grasp the situation better than Pulaski's own countrymen.

In his letter to Pulaski, General Vioménil wrote: "Believe me, Dear Marshal, that I understand very well your case and I shall do all that is in my power to terminate your afflictions. For the time being, please take care of yourself, especially of your health, for your life is needed in the fight for Poland's independence, much more than anything else."

Pulaski, in turn, wrote to others and proved a talented writer when fired. "I have always been against any violence," he declared. "I practiced leniency for the vanquished. While the Russians barbarously treated my countrymen, I set their prisoners free. I commuted death penalty when decreed by the law for hard labor. Why am I to suffer such a great injustice attributed to me?"

Frederick of Prussia started negotiations regarding the partition of Poland, and in February 1772 a temporarily secret agreement between Prussia, Russia and Austria was made. When, in the last effort, on February 2, the confederates occupied Wawel Castle in Kraków, it was but a swan song for the movement. The shadow of the imminent partition of Poland was cast over the whole country. Blamed for an attempt to "murder" the king, the Confederacy began losing popularity and the will for further fighting as well.

Pulaski was among those few who still hoped for a better tomorrow and wanted to continue fighting. With his scrambled army, Casimir pursued from Kraków up north. He joined forces with Kossakowski and together they chased the withdrawing Drevitz, though without a significant effect.

On April 19, Commander Zaremba laid down his weapons. Soon after that, Wawel fell. The rest of the confederates commanded by Radzimiński and Zieliński headed to their last resort, the fortress and monastery of Częstochowa. Pursuing them, an overwhelming Russian army was marching under the command of Suvorov. What other chances were there now? Either to perish under the rubble of the fortress, escape, or commit suicide. Pulaski felt uneasy about these options. While the bombardments and storms continued, the defenders fought bravely, often causing significant losses to the adversaries, but with no hope for victory.

Then, Suvorov called for a cease-fire. To stop the bloodshed, he promised pardon to the confederates. Pulaski took up negotiations. He agreed to hand down the fortress to the representative of the Polish Senate, but only under the following conditions:

1. All resentments caused by the circumstances of war would be forgiven.
2. Fortress Częstochowa would remain a sovereign part of Poland, under a Catholic commander.
3. All soldiers willing to serve would be enlisted in the Polish army.

Suvorov sent a messenger to Warsaw requesting authorization to take over Częstochowa. The top commanders of the Confederacy gathered in Cieszyn, and on May 19, decided upon emigration. Casimir Pulaski sorted out his most faithful soldiers and in changed clothes helped them to leave the besieged fortress. He, himself, dressed like a tradesman, left the Bright Mount of Częstochowa on May 31, 1772, ceding command to Radzimiński and Zieliński.

Now from his wandering road, Pulaski sent a message to the defenders of Częstochowa with the following words:

"I took up the arms for the public's sake, pro publico bono, and for the same sake I must lay them down. The union of three powerful neighbors disabled us of any further defense. The matter, they made me involved in, would make it difficult for me to conduct negotiating capitulation, and bound you all with my misfortune. However, your bravery and dedication assure me about your readiness to serve the Fatherland again, if the circumstances allow it, as well as you served with me. Do not despair! Nil desperandum."

A week later, he wrote again to his Częstochowa crew:

"This is not our last hope. Let us trust in God who never fails. The big potentates have just begun to unite and that may lead to the big war. Only the big war may bring us hope for Independence."

The former star of the anti-Russian uprising, the independent commander of the Confederacy, and a hero known in Europe, was now being held up to public scorn as a perpetrator of attempted regicide. He was tried in absentia, branded a traitor, sentenced to death, and his property was confiscated. By now, the Generality fighters, one by one, were overcome by the Russians. Insurrection under Hetman Ogiński's command in Lithuania was put down by the Russian General Suvorov. The fall of the final confederate outposts of Lanckorona, Tyniec and Częstochowa made it complete.

On the last day of May, 1772, Pulaski slipped out of Częstochowa, making his way across the Silesian border, never to see Poland again. The Confederation of Bar was finished. Approximately 5,000 confederate troops were sent to Siberia, while Bishop Sołtyk, Seweryn Rzewuski, the "prophet" Jandołowicz and others were released from Russian confinement, and returned home.

EXILE

At the beginning of July 1772, Casimir Pulaski, an embittered and disillusioned man, began his exile. Princess Francesca moved into Altwasser, possibly with a view to sheltering him, since in Prussia he was not officially hunted. In early July he was in Dresden, then moved to Frankfurt am Main, where he stayed with Prince Radziwiłł "Panie Kochanku." From there he wrote to the Foreign Minister of France, Prince D'Aiguillon, to request political asylum. While waiting for the reply, Casimir moved back to Dresden, and took ill. The man, accustomed to the hardships of war, the one who often went with little sleep, inadequate food, and never rested, now collapsed. He was feverish, had a chronic headache and was exhausted. His nature could not take idleness. Impatient for his reply, in September he took advantage of Colonel Alexander Lubomirski's traveling to Paris—Lubomirski served in the French army—and traveled with him to inquire about the status of his request. Many influential people supported Casimir's asylum plea. Despite the friendly attitude of the French authorities, wishing to spare him persecution, Casimir learned that no official asylum would be granted.

All bad news came at once. At Częstochowa, negotiations ended and the fortress capitulated on August 18, 1772. The partition treaty, with a third of the Polish territory being divided between Russia, Prussia and Austria, was officially published in Petersburg on August 5, and promulgated all over Europe. Casimir was followed by Russian and Austrian agents and had to change his location constantly to avoid arrest. In Strasbourg, where he stayed with Count Sapieha, he was contemplating relocating to Sweden. An armed conflict between Sweden and Russia was expected at the time but proved to be illusory. He was pushed to the brink of despair, suffocating in the atmosphere where his friends could do little to help and his enemies (he never lacked those) had the upper hand.

With his health improving a bit, Casimir risked once more to see Francesca in Altwasser, where he might also have stayed earlier. There is a documented record he visited her this time in her secluded mansion. He learned from her about his brother Anthony, who after three years of confinement in Kazan as a prisoner of war, had enlisted in the Russian army. Now, he was a free man and, apparently, enjoying excellent relationships with several dignitaries of the Russian empress' court. Casimir took advantage of the circumstance and turned to his brother for help in obtaining the right to return to Poland.

While in Altwasser, the self-confident Pulaski had accompanied Princess Francesca in her carriage to the military parade at Neisse (Nysa) set up for the Prussian Frederick who loved the military drill, parades and reviews. Casimir was recognized there and barely avoided arrest. The event caused diplomatic intervention. King Stanisław August Poniatowski was involved. This resulted in some friction between him and Francesca. It was clear that for security, they had to part.

Upon the receipt of the call from the secretary of the Generality, Bohusz, Pulaski took off for Paris. He traveled incognito through Silesia. Stopping in inns and taverns on his way, he listened to folk tales of the heroic confederates' fights. In Paris, Pulaski met with Bohusz, Wielhorski, the conspiratorial Corsican Rossi, General Vioménil and others.

However, for political reasons, after Minister D'Aiguillon voiced his protest, Casimir could not be invited to the reunion of Polish emigrees at Landshut. It would be impolitic for France to publicly admit sheltering "the king killer," argued the minister. On October 15, 1772, Casimir traveled to Nancy in the company of the well-wishing General Vioménil. On October 29, he addressed again Minister D'Aiguillon and received his consent for staying in Paris until his case pending before the Polish court was resolved. It was expected that the Seym, which had convened in Warsaw at the time, would forgive all confederates and clear Pulaski of his charges.

In early March Pulaski received his long awaited news from Poland but they did not augur well. The suits and accusations filed at court started with "the infamous Pulaski who ordered the event against the king" and "the event" was spelled out "regicide."

Casimir responded by addressing a manifesto to the convening estates.

He wrote: "I desire no favors or good graces. Yes, I do demand to have my case at court and learn what was the crime I am charged with, to be cleared of the charges, and remove the spot contrary to my virtue and yet blackening my reputation." He also declared readiness to appear at court, "covered with the shield of virtue and innocence," to defend himself in person. Luckily, his true friend, Princess Francesca, whom he met in early May near Dresden, talked him out of it.

The trial took place at the Seym court on June 7, 1773, in keeping with all appearences of law and order. Kuźma-Kosiński and Strawiński did not appear at court and nobody insisted on it. Their written testimonies were submitted and accepted as credible. It should be noted that Kuźma-Kosiński who had nobility bestowed on him by the king (hence his second name) with an annual pay of 400 ducats, for years lived in sunny Italy to return only after the third partition to Poland where he died in 1822. Strawiński was also adequately remunerated and, later, found his way to Italy. During the trial he remained under the empress' direct protection. A year a and half after the coup, on April 9, 1773, he deposited at the city council of Wilno a detailed testimony, relating how Pulaski ordered him to kidnap the king and, in case the party would not evade capture, to "deprive him [the king] of life."

On June 30, Pulaski wrote to Seym Speaker Lubomirski to have a counselor-at-law assigned to represent him. His application was voted upon. It was ruled that the counsel would be assigned only if the accused appeared at court in person. Protests were drowned out by applause and the king's intimidating remarks. The king applied to the situation his "lesser evil" lifetime philosophy: "No verdict for the charge of regicide, no amnesty to all those who participated in the Confederacy. Now, you decide."

As the only "eyewitness" the king supported the evidence provided by Kuźma and Strawiński and had a chance to publicize again his "miraculous escape from the hands of the cold-blooded murderers sent by Pulaski."

Casimir Pulaski, in "judgment by default," and imprisoned Walenty Łukawski, were sentenced to death. Łukawski was executed, Pulaski's vindication took place first in 1792, when the Russian Embassy temporarily lost its power in Poland.

The war between Russia and Turkey had dragged on since the fall of 1768. After many bitter and bloody battles, on May 19, 1772, Russia forced Turkey into an armistice, but peace negotiations failed. In the spring of 1773, Russia resumed the hostilities. General Rumyantsov started a new offensive from his headquarters at Jassy with an intention of crossing the River Danube. Then, the western countries, troubled with Russian expansion to the South, decided to help Turkey.

Confident in the Polish "raison d'état," Casimir Pulaski decided to take advantage of the situation and, with the prospect of freeing Poland from foreign occupants, resumed action as well.

At the end of September, Casimir Pulaski moved to Strasbourg and on October 5, he issued a manifesto protesting the verdict imposed upon him. Then, shaking off a sense of fiasco, he recovered from depression and decided to resume new action. Casimir turned to the Generality members, Bohusz, Sapieha and Tarnowski, residing in Strasbourg, for recommendation letters to the Turkish sultan and the grand visier to organize Polish army units in Turkey for a mutual fight against Russia.

For that purpose, he also needed necessary funds. However, none of the Polish magnates were eager to invest in a venture of uncertain success. The most support Casimir Pulaski received was from the least expected, Prince Radziwiłł "Panie Kochanku," who was known as a notorious drunk.

In the meantime, Pulaski watched carefully what was going on at the Russian-Turkish front. He also recruited new soldiers and tried to find new sponsors supporting his initiative. All the more, the Turks made some successful advances at Shumla, Varna and Rushchuk (Ruse). On March 8, 1774, a big farewell dinner was thrown for

Casimir Pulaski's benefit at the seat of the Sapiehas in Paris. He and his officers were leaving the very next day for Turkey.

In Paris, the winter carnival was pro-Polish and balls à la Polonaise were popular. The new polonaise of Michael Ogiński, entitled "Farewell to Fatherland," was frequently played everywhere.

In the group of officers leaving the very next day with Pulaski for Turkey was Joseph Zajączek, later a "Jacobin," general of the Warsaw Duchy and, in the wake of the Vienna Congress, the disgraced tsarist governor in the Kingdom of Poland. He joined the Cofederacy at 17 and then immigrated to France as Michael Wielhorski's assistant. He served Pulaski well as the exact if glorifying chronicler of the Turkish expedition of his very first commander.

TURKISH EXPEDITION

*P*ulaski and the officers traveled separately and took various routes through Austria and Switzerland. They reached Italy and, on April 12, 1774, boarded a ship in Venice and traveled to Ragusa or, what is called today, Dubrovnik. In Ragusa, they reported to the French Consulate to comply with certain formalities, and received that consul's blessing, for France was willing to support the enterprise. Then, they continued further to the camp of the Grand Vizier in Shumla, renamed Kolarovgrad in the Bulgarian People's Republic. In his monograph, Konopczyński precisely traced the route Pulaski took. Casimir Pulaski led his small detachment around Chernogora, via Trebishte, Bilek and many other places like Niš and Sofiya, until they reached Varna in June, and established a camp near that city. Casimir started organizing his new legion and training the volunteers, some of them of Slavic descent, more and more volunteers joining him every day.

It was not easy to operate in Turkey where he had, among other difficulties, to overcome Turkish bureaucracy and even more the prejudice of Muslims, adherents of the religion founded by the prophet Muhammed to whom Christians were "giaours," deserving nothing but contempt. Nevertheless, Grand Vizier Mussin-Zade was friendly and Sultan Abdul Hamid was lavish with promises to help Poland until the final victory. At the beginning, the Turks were doing quite well on the front. They regained almost the entire coast of the River Danube, but they were unable to mount an offensive. For the Poles, the distance to Polish territory was only six days on horseback, but getting there was wishful thinking. Ever optimistic, Pulaski envisaged reaching the city of Bar, declaring insurrection against Russia, and resuming the old plan of a victorious march to Warsaw.

Despite these hopes, the situation on the Russian-Turkish front then tipped in favor of Russia. Field Marshal Rumyantsov had resumed the campaign with a swift maneuver of General Kamienski at Bazargic, seriously threatening the right wing of the Turkish army gathered by Shumla. Now, helping the Turks, Casimir Pulaski had again to confront Suvorov's forces. On June 20, Suvorov attacked the left wing of the Turkish forces at Kozluduy. The Turks fought hard and succeeded in pushing the Russians back to the other side of the River Danube.

The Grand Vizier called Pulaski to the main camp for consultation. Seeing innumerable Turkish forces in good condition: janisaries, bashi-buzouks, Arab spahis, Tartars and Bosnians, he urged the Turks to attack the Russians immediately before the Russians attacked first with greater forces. Unfortunately, the Grand Vizier, an old man weighed down with age, without energy, did not have the stomach for a bold decision. The Turkish army was demoralized by shortages. Robbery was the only way to feed horses that otherwise would starve.

On the very next day, June 29, the Russians crossed the river by Silistra-Gurobala, bringing a large part of their forces, and prepared their attack. The Pulaski legion and the noisy Arabs fought in three counterattacks and caused severe losses. They pushed the Russians back behind the river. The returning soldiers were saluted by a noisy uproar by the Turks, but their joy was premature. The next morning, the Russians appeared again. At the dawn the entire river was covered with rafts and boats full of fresh troops. They easily crossed the river back to the Turkish side and immediately formed numerous compact columns of infantry, marching like living fortresses to the terrible sound of drums. Casimir knew what it meant. Cavalry would not be able to break those live fortresses. They could be held back merely by artillery. He galloped to the Vizier with that piece of advice but no one would listen. When the Russian artillery joined the hostilities, the entire camp panicked. The army ran away in panic. Pulaski and his men were stationed on a hilltop. The Grand Vizier still undecided, their function was to cover up the retreat of the panicked army ready to kill one another to get a horse and escape. That big defeat ended Pulaski's last hopes.

On July 21, 1774, a peace agreement between Russia and Turkey was signed in Kučuk Kaynardzha. It secured freedom for the Tartars and Russian protection for the Orthodox people living on the Turkish territory. Poland was not even mentioned. Although Turkey did not accept the partition of Poland, this had no significant political meaning whatsoever. Frustrated, Pulaski stayed at Adrianople for a while. Then, following the sudden death of the Grand Vizier, Turkish authorities, feeling released from any obligations toward the Polish allies, gave notice that the Polish legion had to leave Turkey within four weeks. Otherwise, Pulaski and his subordinates would be handed over to the Russians. For Casimir Pulaski, it was the time of great trial. He felt responsible for the people who joined his legion. They were all without any money and any support. All desperate requests for help from the English envoy Murray, the French Embassy and other sources had failed. The Turkish authorities recommended that Pulaski move to Rodosto on the Sea of Marmara, where he obtained a little subsidy. Because that was insufficient to satisfy his creditors, Casimir dressed as a Tartar, and together with Joseph Zajączek, escaped Constantinople. From there, they got to Smyrna by boat, under the protection of French Consul Peyssonnel. Here again, Casimir miraculously escaped danger. A Russian warship arrived at Smyrna with an order to catch him just a few hours after Pulaski had left on a small French vessel. The Russians tried to chase him, but a heavy fog over the sea saved his life from Russian revenge.

DEBTORS PRISON AND A NEW HOPE

asimir Pulaski landed in Marseilles, France, in the middle of October, 1774, with Joseph Zajączek and several other legionnaires and castaways. He was penniless. Paradoxically, the heir of many towns and dozens of dozens of villages and the soldier famous all over Europe found himself in extreme poverty. An additional burden was his distress for the fate of his subordinates for whom he felt responsible.

In late December, he petitioned some Polish magnates for help, Ignacy Bohusz among them, and turned to the French Ministry of Foreign Affairs. His petitions brought no immediate relief but, archived, they provide us with a precious historic record.

For his own survival and that of the few around him, Casimir took high-interest loans. He expected to pay them off soon since he had mentioned the money situation writing some time before to his relatives, Prince Radziwiłł "Panie Kochanku" and Princess Francesca, who had never failed him. He felt down and was frank with them. He wrote, "What else is there for me to do? Our education since child forbids raising one's hand against oneself and my hours dragging out in torment do not bring the end so much desired." Instead of help he received the news of his mother's serious illness, the sudden death of his sister Lady Chamberlain Joanna Walewska, and his brother Anthony's misbehavior. There was also news about efforts in Warsaw regarding his vindication process and eventual right to return to Poland. His last letter addressed to the Seym was dated in August, 1776.

His financial obligations had grown to 12,000 liras, equal to 7,000 franks. At the time when Casimir Pulaski was trying, with help from Major Rossi, to apply for service in the American army, he was arrested for his debts. Desperately poor, Casimir shared the prison cell with all kinds of common criminals. Major Rossi and other friends tried to intervene to provide him at least with better accommodations in prison, but they had no success. He was to be released only under the condition that his debt would be paid off in full. His creditors did not want securities, persuasions and other guaranties offered. Desperate letters were dispatched to his mother, Marianna Pulaska, his sister, Anna, to Princess Francesca, former Generality bosses, and other more or less friendly persons.

Finally, the money arrived. Princess Teofila Sapieha, a dedicated supporter of the Confederacy, joined the action. Energetic as ever, she turned directly to the Marsailles banker Saltz and had Pulaski released on bail quickly.

Joseph Zajączek had left Casimir's service before the trouble and had enlisted in the French army as a lieutenant. Casimir Pulaski, with the stigma of regicide, had no chance to serve in any European army, either French or Spanish, where he tried to enter.

Upon his release, Pulaski met and became friends with Claude de Rulhière, a writer, historian and mason, who was ever eager to discuss politics. The result of that association was an extensive publication in French about the Bar Confederacy, entitled: "L'Histoire de l'Anarchie de Pologne" ("The History of Anarchy in Poland"). The book was not the only positive effect of Pulaski's acquaintance with de Rulhière. Rulhière brought Pulaski to meet Benjamin Franklin, ending this hopelessly passive period in Pulaski's life.

On July 26, 1776, Pulaski wrote to Silas Deane, American diplomat, offering his service to the colonies in America. Shortly after that, Rulhière introduced Casimir Pulaski to Benjamin Franklin. The man in black, a representative of the American Continental Congress in Paris, was the one who "stole thunder from the Heavens, and scepters from tyrants." Franklin recognized the true value of the gallant young man, his military experience and his courage. He realized that all these assets could be useful to the cause, their fight for freedom. On May 29, 1777, Mr. Franklin penned a letter to the Commander-in-Chief, General George Washington and handed it to Pulaski.

The letter is now kept in the U.S. National Archives in Washington, D.C. It read, "Count Pulaski of Poland, an Officer famous throughout Europe for his Bravery and Conduct in Defense of Liberties of his Country, against the three great invading Powers of Russia, Austria and Prussia, will have the Honor of delivering this into your Excellency's Hands. The Court here have encouraged and promoted his Voyage, from an Opinion that he may be highly useful in our Service."

From the beginning of June 1777, Pulaski waited in Nantes for the ship to take him to America. He worried that something might unexpectedly happen and ruin his only hope of starting a new life in the New World. He ended his letter to his sister Anna asking for prayers for the dead. He knew that the English would do everything possible to stop the ship from carrying supplies to the American rebels. A touch of optimism in this sad letter was his listing of addresses for correspondence under care of:

- Claude de Rulhière, author of "History ot Anarchy in Poland," mentioned earlier,
- Pierre de Beaumarchais, author of the "The Barber of Seville," and
- Teresa Potocka, whose court title, Lady Royal Cutter, was mentioned.

The latter, he wrote, was "kind enough to make a promise to pay me attention in Warsaw."

This mention underscored his interest in continuing activities toward his vindication. He never lost his trust in the final victory of truth and justice.

Finally, on June 6, 1777, the American brig "Massachusetts" loaded with supplies and munitions left from the wide mouth of the River Loire for her voyage across the Atlantic. Casimir Pulaski stood silently on board, with four other Poles and several Frenchmen, watching the vanishing lights of the harbor, each lost in his own thoughts.

Pulaski regarded his service in the American army as his only chance. During his two years in exile he learned that as a declared enemy of the three partitioning powers and with the stigma of "king-killer," he was condemned in Europe to a limited sphere of action, below his aspirations.

Casimir cherished the American struggle for independence. The colonists' aspiration to get rid of a foreign yoke was understandable and close to his heart. It also satisfied the personal ambitions of the one who aimed high.

The voyage to America was very long and onerous although the ship in those days was one of the fast ones. On July 23, after traveling for 48 days, the fatigued, creaking "Massachusetts" entered the harbor at Marblehead, near Boston. She was lucky to avoid British warships. Fortunately enough, the cannons stored under the deck were not used. Only the sails on three masts were seriously weakened and the unusual number of mice damaged some of Casimir's English language handbooks and dictionaries hoarded before the voyage.

PULASKI IN AMERICA
BRANDYWINE, GERMANTOWN

asimir Pulaski joined the fight against the British in mid-year, 1777, a time considered crucial for the American Revolution. The American Army was basically a revolutionary force consisting mostly of volunteers and could use professional guidance. Even so, Continental Congress had an overload of business, from trifles to all-important matters, and was late assigning appointments.

Major-General William Heath, commander of Boston, made a brief note in his diary under the date of July 26, 1777: "Count Pulaski, a nobleman from Poland, arrived in Boston, we dined at the headquarters."

Casimir Pulaski had disembarked at Marblehead Harbor, north of Boston, three day earlier. Tired by the 48-day voyage, he was dazed by the English, a language that was foreign to him. For the first time he experienced the language barrier, which shut him out from people he was meeting. With his schooling and exposure to many languages spoken within the Polish Commonwealth, he could easily communicate with people in the countries he had visited so far. His primary need was to master the language since he was as much a man of the pen as of the saber.

According to his first informant, the Boston commander, the overall situation on the front was quite precarious. The English had just occupied New York and battles were in progress along the Hudson River and Lake Champlain threatening Philadelphia, the

Colonial capital and the nest of rebels. Sir William Howe was about to strike against Philadelphia and General John Burgoyne, who had captured Fort Ticonderoga, was moving south toward Albany.

With a great deal of interest, Casimir Pulaski reviewed American troops and found them very different from the European troops. They consisted of 11,000 men, dirt-poor and inadequately armed. The majority wore loose, gray hunting jackets, and the others wore homespun shirts. These particular units, without any military drill, were formed in a double-row, with the short on the front and the tall behind them. However, it was understood by the former Marshal of Łomża that these troops had been hurriedly collected and made up of volunteers.

Pulaski's first adventure in writing on American topics, if still in French, was a memorandum he prepared for his old comrade-in-arms from the Bar Confederacy, Maurycy Beniowski. On July 28, 1777, he addressed Commissioners Franklin and Deane in Paris on behalf of the famous adventurer of Madagascar, to sponsor an expedition. It was a failed gesture of friendship because the enterprise certainly was not in the United Colonies' sphere of influence or interest.

It was the Age of Enlightenment, French public opinion was supportive of the struggle of Americans for liberty against the tyranny of England's George III. However, the American colonies were a mixed bag. They were divided not only regionally, as each was a separate entity, but the public was split between Patriots and Loyalists.

Also, there was remarkable disparity in economic and military resources among the colonies. All the more, the guerilla-style Indians and conscientious-objective Quakers were, by accident, supporting the Loyalists, not the Rebels. Also, the war was dragging on for many years, with some victories and some defeats. All that caused raging inflation, intense civilian suffering and disappointments. In addition, there was a lack of enthusiasm and a measure of resistance on the part of the civil authorities to the military command.

The Continental Army was desperately short of men, they even thought of using slaves as soldiers. Patrick Henry's "give me liberty or give me death" would be helpless against a Negro insurrection.

Caring more for their personal liberty than for the sovereignty of the colonies, the blacks in the South joined the Royal Army, which promised them freedom on victory.

In August, General George Washington, the Commander-in-Chief, kept close to the York Road, sending out reconnoiterers to discover where the British navy would strike.

His Neshaminy Creek camp (now Warwick Township), 20 miles north of Philadelphia, with the headquarters in the Molan House (now a Museum), was his longest encampment. It lasted 13 days (August 10-23, 1777) and it was there that Pulaski found the Commander-in-Chief on August 21.

The brash, young Marquis de LaFayette, a very wealthy relative of the King and Queen of France, was already there. He joined General Washington at his headquarters on August 19. The marquis' offer of his services to the Continental Army was a windfall to the Commander-in-Chief because the French alliance was of upmost importance in Washington's eyes and a much needed morale booster.

Washington's military campaigns in the area of Philadelphia and Horatio Gates's victory over Burgoyne at Saratoga, with the help of Thaddeus Kosciuszko's fortifications, convinced the French that the Continentals were a match for the British. This made them inclined to recognize the new nation and conclude an alliance.

Initially, General Washington was not too excited about meeting still another European nobleman looking for glory and demanding a command.

He was politely and "ex officio" taciturn until Pulaski awoke Washington's interest with his idea of creating mounted troops or dragoons, enlisting English prisoners-of-war in the army, and partisan warfare on a large scale.

He also suggested interrupting communication lines between Fort Ticonderoga (lost to Burgoyne on July 6, 1777) and the British Army by building a chain of small, well-fortified posts operated by skillful supporters. Apparently, Washington became interested, and directed Casimir to Congress with his letter of recommendation.

In compliance with General Washington's wishes, Pulaski presented the letters of recommendation to Congress and his own on August 24, 1777. He mentioned his four-year experience: "I did go through the hardship of war in Poland," he wrote. "In Poland I commanded 1,800 men in different battles... The sieges and attacks of Places which I have managed, give one a title to be counted among men of military experience ...I have passed hither from Europe to do myself the Honor of being admitted worthy of Citizens in the defense of Their Country and Their Liberty... I would like to obtain a position directly under the Commander-in-Chief... If that cannot be, yet joined to the Marquis de LaFayette... I would take pleasure in sharing his labours and executing the orders of the Commander-in-Chief as subaltern of the marquis... Above all, the most important thing for me is to be near the enemy and have a chance to prove my abilities as a good officer."

George Washington supported his application to the president of the Continental Congress, John Hancock, writing, "Sir, I do myself the Honor to enclose you a copy of Dr. Franklin's Letter in favor of Count Pulaski from Poland, by whom this will be handed to you. Some time ago I had a letter from Mr. Deane, couched in terms equally favorable to the Character and Military Abilities of this Gentleman."

The next recommendation letter Washington sent to Congressman George Clymer of Philadelphia, where Pulaski was directed.

Casimir also brought recommendation letters for him to General LaFayette, together with private correspondence from LaFayette's beautiful wife Adrienne. His thoughtfulness pleased General LaFayette very much. They soon became close friends and LaFayette introduced Pulaski to other officers. While waiting for his nomination, Pulaski and several other Poles in his company, temporarily stayed with LaFayette's staff. Casimir did not waste time. He paid visits to some of the Congressmen and presented them with the following words: "Gentlemen, your commissioners wrote to you in my favor. I will do my best to confirm their opinion, as much as my abilities and the trust in me would allow. I would like to be assigned to a company of volunteers on horseback, in the rank entitling me to command the whole division, if I deserve it." Signed: "Casimir Victor Count Korvin Pulaski."

In America, Pulaski preferred to use his well-known title, though with discretion, at least on paper. On September 5, still only a volunteer, Pulaski was invited to a tactical staff conference, presided over by Washington.

BRANDYWINE

General William Howe landed his British forces on August 25. General Washington had to protect the continental capital of Philadelphia more for political than strategic reasons. For two weeks he kept a close watch on the advancing foe and was ready and willing to give General Howe a battle at the fords of the Brandywine. Until the Battle of Brandywine, military action was limited to skirmishes.

On September 9, the American Army occupied a position on the north bank of the creek. A grand division under General Charles Lord Cornwallis crossed the Brandywine upstream at Chad's Ford and moved around, intending to attack the Americans from the rear or on the flank, hoping to repeat the successful British maneuver executed at the Battle of Long Island. When the British struck, the Americans were caught while changing flanks, and men under Commander John Sullivan retreated in confusion.

On September 11, 1777, the big confrontation with the English army of General Howe took place at the marshy area on the Brandywine Creek between Chester and Philadelphia. It was a test of Pulaski's skill as a good cavalry officer (even though he was the foreigner and a papist). The battle was on difficult terrain, in a forest of shrubs and trees in the morning fog. American soldiers, some of them barefoot, marched spiritedly. singing the popular "Yankee-Doodle." Their commanders fought courageously. Commander Thomas Conway, an Irishman who once served France, directed his 800 men in a most brilliant manner. Prompt aid from General Nathanael Greene saved Sullivan's forces from total destruction. In spite of their bravery, the English and hired Hessians had the advantage of good training over American enthusiasm. LaFayette sustained a leg wound while rallying the troops, and made his escape thanks to his aide-de-camp. Then, while attempting to rally the fugitives, LaFayette was taken prisoner. The enemy suffered big losses, but still was able to push the insurgents back to the river.

Casimir Pulaski most likely kept close to Washington and his staff, possibly reconnoitering with them before the battle. As he had no commission, his status was that of a volunteer. In the face of American defeat at the hands of General Howe, and still without a commission, Pulaski was worried about supplies being cut off.

He asked Washington for immediate command over a small 30-horseman headquarters cavalry detachment for the counterattack. He received permission. With his usual intrepidity and sharp judgment, shouting commands in a mixture of English, French and Polish, he led the charge in a swift maneuver. For a while this confused the British, taken by the boldness of his move. It retarded the enemy's advance and resulted in a brief delay, allowing the Americans a successful withdrawal.

Furthermore, Pulaski perceived that the enemy was maneuvering to take possession of the road leading to Chester, with an eye on cutting American retreat, or at least their column with baggage.

Casimir hastened to General Washington to communicate the information, and was immediately authorized by the Commander-in-Chief to collect the scattered troops on hand, and make the best of them.

Pulaski, by an oblique advance upon the enemy's front and right flank, defeated their objective, and effectively protected both the baggage column and the American retreat. The battle was lost, but the Americans withdrew toward Chester, suffering fewer losses than the British. It was hardly a Pyrrhic victory for the English. Unreliable and confused intelligence was chiefly blamed for the American defeat.

Casimir's excellent orientation in the battle, courage and bravery brought him recognition among officers, including his friend, Captain Paul Bentalou, who as a diarist and eyewitness rendered an authentic account of that and other actions. Despite critical arguments of Pulaski's adversary, Judge William Johnson, Casimir Pulaski was indeed the most talented and experienced general of that war. He also proved to be an excellent strategist and tactician.

On September 15, 1777, the Continental Congress recognized Pulaski's valor, personal courage, and his ability to command, and voted to commission him a Brigadier-General and Commander of American cavalry. Washington published the order of Pulaski's appointment on September 21 and commanded the new general to begin the task of creating an efficient cavalry force.

Factually, at that time, the entire American cavalry consisted of 727 men in four cavalry regiments, dispersed between other formations and used as reconnaissance detachments. They were neither well trained nor at full strength. Also, the colonial forces were in the habit of using details of men and horses from the cavalry for numerous other purposes like generals' escorts or orderlies. Under these circumstances, it was a Herculean task for Pulaski to train and discipline a disheartened group of soldiers, including some foreigners among the officers and privates. Despite the difficulties, the cavalry section organized by Pulaski after his appointment, if not big, was distinctive.

The Americans were still retreating, when the British under General Howe entered Philadelphia. Very soon, the entire city fell into British hands and the American insurgents were forced to withdraw. In the difficult situation, with constant evacuation of headquarters, archives, hospitals and the like, Pulaski's main duty was to cut supplies to the English troops occupying Philadelphia and to direct them to the American insurrectionists. The British paid for their food supplies in pure gold, while the Americans could only afford to pay in worthless paper bills. Therefore, the farmers, despite prohibition, were tempted by the gold and supplied all kinds of goods to the city by the wagonload. Casimir tracked out the secret passage at Frankford Creek near Kensington and intercepted these supplies.

At the beginning of October 1777, General Washington attacked Philadelphia. In that campaign, Pulaski fought several skirmishes with the English army headed by Generals Howe and Cornwallis.

His regiments were depleted during the weeks prior to the battle of Germantown. The day before the main engagement, Casimir commanded no more than a small scouting force, inadequate for his task.

GERMANTOWN

On October 3, 1777, Washington moved his headquarters back to Nashaminy Creek. The army knew about General Gates' success against Burgoyne. An appeal was made to arouse the ambition of every man in the main army to not be outdone by his northern brethren. The soldiers also knew that, as General Howe's amnesty expired, what was left was 'conquest or death.' Washington's decision was to finish Howe by a single stroke of genius.

The Delaware River fords blocked British supply ships. British forces were split into two parts, with the main body in Germantown and the rest under Cornwallis in Philadelphia, about five miles away. Washington, prone to quick and risky action, was cautious enough this time to seek the opinions of his general officers.

The majority of them agreed that this was a favorable opportunity to launch an attack. The Americans previously had been posted around Germantown and had some familiarity with the area. The American Army had about 8,000 Continentals and 3,000 volunteer militia. The British forces were estimated at about 9,000. For some unknown reason, the initial plan of attack elaborated by Washington was changed, most likely at the last moment.

This second plan called for commanders Stephen, Greene and McDougall to make an unnecessary encirclement and attack the British right and center, leaving the left for Armstrong's militia. Through a successful and synchronized attack Washington hoped to push the British into the Schuylkill River. Germantown was a village along a road two miles long. The British line of encampment crossed at right angles. Washington's columns of Wayne, Sullivan and Conway did not reach Chestnut Hill until sunrise, marching from where Skippack Road led straight to the enemy camp.

From sources, it appears that Washington's attack at Germantown, that initially was extremely successful, did not surprise the British, who might have been informed by a spy. After its first surprise attack, the British picket line got reinforced by light infantry. Sullivan ordered Conway to form his brigade to aid attacking regiments and to repulse the light infantry. Wayne was dispatched to Sulivan's left, taking the position where Greene was expected.

According to Wayne, he pushed the enemy nearly three miles and was in possession of their whole encampment, when a large body of troops advanced on his left flank. American troops began suddenly to retreat and entirely left the field in spite of every effort that could be made to rally them.

The battle at Germantown, with all the ingredients for an American victory, which possibly would have ended the war, ended in defeat due to mistakes, chaos, mixed orders, and fog that accounted for poor visibility.

Legend says that an extremely tired army camped and fell asleep by the campfire. As per his custom, Casimir Pulaski, with a small detachment, searched the vicinity. During this reconnaissance, he encountered sentinel of General Howe's army. Pulaski ordered his men to feign a counter-attack while he galloped to the headquarters to alert the command. He reported the urgency of seeing General Washington at once. He awakened Aide-de camp, Alexander Hamilton, who tried to make skeptical remarks. Awakened by loud verbal exchange, the Commander-in-Chief stood in the doorway of his tent and listened to Casimir's report. An alarm was ordered immediately and Pulaski, with several hundred soldiers, rushed and beat the enemy back. This saved the brigade commanded by Washington. The other two brigades, under Wayne and Smallwood, were overthrown. The first one was destroyed and the other dispersed in confusion and disorder. Allegedly, the panicked Americans literally fled from their own victory. Pulaski was barely able to cover their retreat.

The Americans were able to withdraw, and Howe, as usual, did not pursue energetically. After Germantown, in view of the fact that

Philadelphia remained in the hands of the British, American generals decided to suspend military action and retire for the winter at Valley Forge. Pulaski, who during four winters in Poland had learned winter warfare, presented his different viewpoint in writing. His argument was that the winter inactivity would demoralize the troops and ruin the army while, on the other hand, activity would harden people and train soldiers for war's hardship. Also, it would strengthen morale and attract the allies.

The respite in military operations did not suit Pulaski's urge to constantly harass the enemy. He continually conducted raids on the British around Philadelphia. Thus, at the skirmish of Chestnut Hill on November 23, when the French commander Charles Armand Tuffin engaged the British forces, Pulaski took command with his cavalry and turned into victory what could have been an American defeat.

Alas, the winter came quickly, the rain turned roads into swamps, wet gunpowder turned into black grease. Soldiers were hastily accommodated in provisional barracks or shacks with no heating. There was a shortage of everything: clothing, shoes, blankets, food and even bread. Horses died from starvation. Supply wagons had to be drawn by men. Pulaski, too, stayed in a shabby farmhouse in a similar situation.

Despite all this, Pulaski did not waste his time, but utilized it on reconnaissance and to write letters to General Washington and Congress, offering his viewpoints and suggestions about the manner of further running the liberation war.

Considering that the English army employed foreigners, Pulaski proposed enlisting young prisoners of war into the insurrection army. Those who resisted, could be sent to work on farms. To further increase the manpower, Casimir suggested that the ship captains be authorized to recruit young men from Europe, especially from Poland and France. Again and again, he stressed the necessity of creating a strong American cavalry but his views had mostly been neglected by the American High Command.

These ideas preoccupied Casimir Pulaski over the Christmas season spent at Valley Forge. Conditions there were miserable, log huts for soldiers had insufficient straw to cover floors, and food came at starvation rations, with no fodder for horses. Many horses died and were butchered for meat. The dark days at Valley Forge were brightened by the visit of Washington's wife, Martha, along with other prominent ladies. She attracted to her husband's quarters LaFayette and other foreign officers, including the gallant Pulaski.

On New Year's Eve, Washington ordered Pulaski to move his scanty cavalry from Valley Forge to Trenton, New Jersey, and to train his troops in preparation for the spring campaign. Casimir and his horsemen reached Trenton on January 8, 1778. The two winter months, January and February, were a struggle: the men were unpaid, supplies were not forthcoming. There was no fodder for the horses and Pulaski was forbidden to make requisitions. The request to stay near the enemy's line was granted not to Pulaski who earnestly solicited it, but to Captain Allen Maclean. Nevertheless, Pulaski continued to be full of hope that his big days were still ahead, and continued organizing and training the cavalry.

In the meantime, Washington ordered Pulaski to aid General Anthony Wayne at Mount Holly, New Jersey, in his encounter with a large British force. The battle of March 1, 1778, ended in an American victory, and several hundred head of cattle, which the British had requisitioned from the farmers, were saved for use by the continental troops.

Pulaski was hurt by Washington's accusation of overtaxing the cavalry and relaying the complaints of officers about "severe duty." All that compounded Pulaski's difficulties. Disappointed, Casimir began to consider his resignation as commander of the horse, seeking instead a position in which he could establish a force consisting of infantry and cavalry, independent from other generals.

COMMANDER OF AMERICAN CAVALRY

*T*renton was supposed to become the birthplace of the American cavalry. Pulaski got his appointment and moved with his men shortly after Christmas. He was happy about the move and trusted that the day of grand accomplishments was at hand. Shortly after his arrival, on January 12, 1778, he issued a proclamation to the Trentonians, appealing for greater generosity on objectives relating to the conduct of war. He kept up correspondence persistently with the General-in-Chief and Congress concerning the cavalry.

Initially, Pulaski's proposition to introduce a light cavalry armed with lances or lancemen—a weapon unknown to the Americans—found quiet acceptance. However, when the cost was revealed, Congress failed to approve any more expenses. Pulaski felt that his best plans were crushed.

On February 19, he wrote to Congress: "I have the mortification to see my best projects frustrated by some circumstance or other... In view of this fact, I am compelled to ask for my salary, which I intend to use to equip my detachment at my cost... Be so kind and do me the Honor of answering this letter and two other letters I had the Honor of sending."

In the meantime, Casimir inspected troops stationed in neighboring towns of Flemington and Pennytown, experiencing first hand their misery. Their situation was below the poverty level: with no forage, the quarters occupied by sailors, poor horses not worth their fodder, no firewood and people complaining about the dismantling of fences by soldiers for wood. The soldiers' uniforms were in tatters and their weapons were pathetic. As mentioned before, this scanty cavalry of 727 men was divided among four regiments, headed by Bland, Moylan, Sheldon and Baylor. The ratio was one cavalryman per 25 infantrymen. In that situation, the horsemen played only an auxiliary role for the infantry, conducting reconnaissance, front or rear guard, reconnoitering and serving as generals' escorts and orderlies for staff officers.

Pulaski's idea was to arm dragoons with light lances, improve their performance and bring the American cavalry up to the standards of Europe. "If we had a powerful cavalry, the enemy would not dare to break up and scatter their forces," he used to say. These were empty arguments, not only because of the lack of military imagination but primarily because the funds were lacking.

As a general cavalry inspector, he related poorly with his subordinates, specifically Moylan who was brought to court for unseating Casimir's cousin on his mother's side, Ignatz (John) Zieliński.

Between these problems and conflicts, occasional fights with the enemy were interspersed. For the restless Casimir, they offered a kind of consolation. Both "The Trenton Press" and "New Jersey Journal" published articles occasionally describing Pulaski's mobility and tactical achievements on the battleground. An anonymous correspondent reported:

"Last Friday, Count Pulaski left Trenton at the head of his cavalry which was in top condition, to join with the troops under General Wayne. Judging by his previous exploits, his valor and mobility, he will teach the enemy's calvary a lesson if only he is not deprived of the pleasure by their rapid escape."

One time, when Casimir's detachment was moving along the Delaware River from the Trenton camp, around Camden they happened to come across a large British expedition of 1,200 well armed men, plundering the vicinity and collecting supplies for Philadelphia located across the river. In that situation, General Wayne simulated an insurgent camp at another place close by and with this maneuver he confused the enemy. The battle was fought at Haddonfield on St. Casimir's day. Happy for the occasion to prove himself in battle, Pulaski attacked the British with a great fury and efficiency. The English would have been wiped out if Pulaski's horse was not killed under him or if Wayne were really that "mad Tony" of his reputation and followed the enemy with fierceness demanded by Pulaski.

The press praised the soldiers for bravery, mentioning the number of English casualties. Pulaski got into the article as the one who had his horse killed under him and his success was not depicted in exaggerated terms.

The battle report printed in the "New Jersey Gazette" on March 11, 1778, was colorful, but not very sympathetic for Casimir. "... Though they knew our inferiority of number, our attacking them with a few light horse at Haddonfield, under the command of Brigadier General Count Pulaski, made their fears get the better of their knowledge, as well as their courage, and happiest was the Briton who had the longest legs and the nimblest heads. Leaving bag and baggage, they retreated precipitately to Cooper's Ferry. Pulaski charged right in the middle of the enemy's thicket and this emboldened them towards the aim that was to them unreachable, dispersed them and chased into the river..."

In his report of March 5, 1778, General Wayne expressed fascination with Pulaski's performance despite his risk-taking and bravura, found unacceptable by other American generals.

Discouraged by limitations imposed upon him, the language barrier, and difficulty cooperating with subordinates of mixed origins, Casimir reached a courageous decision. He applied for his resignation as commander of the horse. Instead, Casimir would seek a position in which he could command an independent mixed force consisting of infantry and cavalry.

On March 3, 1778, General Washington accepted Pulaski's dismissal in an elegant tone, stating: "Your intention to resign is founded on reasons which, I presume, make you think the measure necessary. I can only say, therefore, that it will always give me pleasure to bear testimony to the zeal and bravery which you displayed on every occasion. I wish to admit, that proper steps are taken towards improvement of the cavalry and it should be action-ready for the new campaign."

Casimir Pulaski's resignation from the position of cavalry commander did not imply lesser zeal to fight for American independence.

In the middle of March, 1778, Casimir most likely moved from Valley Forge to Yorktown where he joined General Horatio Gates, known to be a close friend of the democratic Pole, Thaddeus Kosciuszko. At that time, Kosciuszko was at York. Even though this link through General Gates would be enough to undermine the general disbelief that the two famous Polish generals and heroes of the American war for independence have had a chance to meet or even learn about each other. True, they could never be friends, separated as they were by temperaments and political views they had developed in Poland. It is uncontestable that despite different temperaments and political backgrounds, they could have met and cooperated to some degree with each other.

Thaddeus Kosciuszko was a son of an impoverished Polish family of noble background. He was a skilled military engineer trained in Poland and France, who offered his services to the Continental Congress at the outbreak of the Revolutionary War in 1776 and was commissioned as Colonel of Engineers in the Continental Army. He was assigned to General Gates heading the Northern Army with headquarters in Albany, New York. Kosciuszko contributed greatly to the General Gates's victory at Saratoga fortifying the American lines, selecting their positions and entrenching them to make them virtually impenetrable and resistant to British attacks.

The successful Commander of the Saratoga Battle was then the Minister of War. Possibly with General Gates's knowledge—and that could have implied Kosciuszko's knowledge—Pulaski formulated a petition relating to the formation of an independent corps of mixed infantry-cavalry partisan troops. On March 19, 1778, Pulaski addressed his petition to the Board of War, in which he wrote:

"The duty of this corps (Legion), placed under my command, will be always to observe, very close at hand, all the movements of the enemy, and take upon the Commander-in-Chief different enterprises, of the nature of surprises, ambuscades, affairs of posts, rearguards, protecting flanks and to advise the Commander-in Chief of the army, and the Board of War, of everything which would be of interest... The corps will be recruited from the people of the country, from deserters, and from prisoners of war, which is agreeable to General George Washington."

The Board of War, which was headed by General Horatio Gates, responded positively to Pulaski's proposal and decided on the formation of that Legion with Casimir Pulaski as the commander in the rank of Brigadier-General.

INDEPENDENT LEGION
CHARLESTON

*O*n March 28, 1778 Congress approved the formation of a separate cavalry entity, the "Pulaski Legion," which was to be composed of 68 cavalrymen and 200 infantrymen under Casimir's command. In addition, the sum of $105,000 was appropriated for equipping the legion. Besides furnishing each new soldier with clothing and weapons from his own pocket, Pulaski was supposed to spend, from that money, $130 for each new soldier.

Every infantryman had to receive one rifle, cap, pair of trousers, two pair of shoes, a comb, three pairs of socks and a jacket. Every cavalryman, in addition, would receive a lance, saddle, boots, horsecomb, "mantelzak" and a rope to tie up the horse. However, the funds were delayed in arriving, and Pulaski used his own money to defray the legion's immediate expenses.

Casimir selected Colonel Michael Kovatch and Lt. Colonel Charles Baron de Bose, Major Count Julius de Monfort and his presumed cousin, Captain Ignatz (John) Zieliński as his officers.

During the five months, between May and October, the Legion was recruited and trained in Baltimore, Maryland. It was now composed of 330 soldiers, 62 more than originally authorized by Congress, and was supposed to be exceptional and exemplary. On April 23, 1778, the "New Jersey Gazette," announced the recruitment to that Corps, which was to be patterned after the Roman Legions.

Not everything was proceeding smoothly during the Legion's organization. General Smallwood had an oversupply of officers and a shortage of privates, who were deserting to Pulaski's Legion. He complained to Washington and Casimir had to return them. Also, the Legion's soldiers somehow fell into conflict with the Corps created to perform guard duty and conduct training schools for young men in the art of war.

While organizing his corps, Pulaski found relaxation in Bethlehem, a settlement of Moravian brothers and sisters in Northampton County, about fifty miles from Philadelphia. On May 18, 1778, Pulaski was visiting General LaFayette, who was recuperating from his Brandywine wound in a hospital in Bethlehem, Pennsylvania. During this visit, Casimir received a crimson silk banner with yellow threads for his Legion, made by Moravian women who were famed for their embroidery. One side of it read: "US" (United States) and a Latin sentence "Unitas Virtus Fortior" (United Valor is Stronger). On the other side was the "Eye of Providence," a Christian and Masonic symbol, encircled by 13 stars and the inscription: "Non Alius Regit" (No Other Governs). That banner stayed with the Legion until Casimir's death, and now it is on display at the Historical Museum in Baltimore, Maryland, and a replica is in the possession of the Polish National Alliance in Chicago.

It was not entirely recruitment and formation. Once, during that period, General Wayne was surrounded by 3,000 British troops near New Jersey. Pulaski rushed to the rescue, and quickly defeated the enemy. His brilliant tactics and bravery amazed General Wayne. On the 29th of July Pulaski held a review of his corps for the Marylanders and on he 15th of September, 1778, he reported to General Washington from Baltimore that the Legion was ready to fight.

At the beginning of October, General Washington assigned Pulaski's Legion to defend a sea base located near New York. Although the Revolutionary force had no navy, privateering flourished. Private brigs and vessels could have been converted any time into a "pirate armada," dangerous to the British. On October 4, Washington ordered Pulaski to rush to Egg Harbor on the New Jersey coast to take part in an expected engagement with the British heading in that direction. On October 8, 1778, the Legion arrived at this location, and two days later the action began. Unfortunately, a deserter named Gustav Juliet informed the commander of the

English expedition, Captain Ferguson, where Pulaski's troops were encamped. Overnight on October 14, the British 400-man landing operation on the island Osborne took the Legion's commander by complete surprise. Some 25 or 30 infantrymen, including Casimir's deputy, Colonel Charles de Bose, were killed.

When the noise aroused Pulaski, he hurriedly gathered the cavalry and with only a slight delay, he swiftly beat the enemy, and forced the British to retreat. However, in the eyes of Congress, the Legion formed to some extent from defectors of the English army, lost its reputation.

After remaining in Egg Harbor for a few days, Pulaski was ordered by Congress to transfer his Legion to Sussex Court House, to reorganize the infantry and to secure new recruits. There, he awaited further orders from General Washington.

On November 10, 1778, Pulaski was ordered to take his Legion to the Minisink settlement on the bank of the Delaware River near Cole's Fort, and take action against Indians whom the British used in fighting against the insurgents.

Casimir was not enthusiastic about this mission. Militarily, it was the wrong mission for the wrong unit. Casimir considered the Indians not worth fighting. Even a victory over them would bring no honor. It was against his idea of chivalry. He was too restless a fighter to do garrison duty or protectionist defense.

He had come to fight the British, to hit, to strike, and strike again in the manner of cavalry warriors. He was a dashing cavalry leader with no place to dash in the Minisink forests. In such a mood of despair and frustration, Pulaski saw no future in continuing. Though the expedition against Indians never took place, it was the last drop of bitterness resulting in Casimir's request for resignation again, on the grounds of his intended return to Europe.

In view of approaching conflict between Poland's neighbors Austria and Prussia, Casimir expected to find there more chances of better serving his country in the struggle of regaining independence.

On Washington's order Pulaski moved to Easton, Pennsylvania, where, discouraged and impatient, on November 15, 1778, he wrote to Washington: "Sir, According to your instruction I will march towards Cole's Fort, but will stop at Rosegrantz to refresh the horses, and will await your further orders. I hope that after returning the Legion to its place and bringing it into good order, I shall have your permission to go to Philadelphia to arrange embarkation. My only wish is to leave the Legion in good condition, that it would remind citizens of this country of my name."

At that time, back in Poland, his brother Anthony had worked hard for months on a resolution that was finally issued by the Seym in fall of 1778, allowing Casimir to come to Warsaw to be vindicated from the accusation of "regicide."

Paradoxically, Casimir Pulaski was a noble gentleman, one of the conservative Polish gentry, a very honest person, and who in large part, financed his Legion from his own pocket.

The money he used was sent him by relatives in Poland with the help of a middleman, a cooperative Polish Jew, Haym Salmon. The same man was a creditor of Thaddeus Kosciuszko.

Surrounded by some people who served in the war for profit, he was accused by them of similar motivation. Much too busy most of the time with fighting war in the field, Pulaski had inadvertently overlooked the bookkeeping of his detachment. In addition, complaints from the part of the population that was not supportive of the insurrection, had worsened the situation.

Then the Congress assigned auditors who angered Casimir, because instead of fighting enemies in the field he had to waste time by clarifying insignificant expenses made in paper money of little value. All that caused Pulaski's belated military action against the British who, in January 1779, occupied the town of Savannah.

Casimir Pulaski, eager to fight the enemy, withdrew his request for resignation. On February 2, Washington ordered Pulaski's Legion to prepare to move southward and join the Corps under the command of General Benjamin Lincoln who, in turn, ordered Pulaski's Legion to march south to South Carolina.

Lincoln's career was remarkable. A farmer born in 1733, he was a lieutenant colonel of the militia at the beginning of the

110

Revolutionary War and hurried to Cambridge, Massachusetts, with other Minutemen at the outbreak of fighting. A good officer, he was steadily promoted, advancing to major general in the Massachusetts militia in 1776. Given command of the Massachusetts troops sent to reinforce New York City in September 1776, he impressed General Washington with his ability. He was appointed a Major-General in the Continental Army in February, 1777, and commanded the New England militia in the defeat of British.

In the middle of March, 1779, the part of Casimir's Legion consisting of infantry, commanded by Colonel Kovatch, left York and headed to South Carolina. Pulaski was detained by the controllers who ardently exercised the prerogatives vested in them by the suspicious Congress.

CHARLESTON

In the spring of 1779, Pulaski was ordered to march his legion from their winter quarters in New Jersey, then recently invaded by the enemy, to Georgia. By the time they reached Williamsburg, then the seat of government in Virginia, a small British fleet had entered the James River and landed some troops.

Jefferson had just succeeded Patrick Henry as the governor of the state. Local skirmishes and other circumstances retarded the march of Pulaski's Legion until the enemy had retreated. Then, Casimir with the rest of his legion reached Charleston, on May 8, three days before the arrival of British General Prevost. Pulaski joined with his second in command Colonel Kovatch, at the same time as General Moultrie, chased by a multitude of British troops, approached Charleston. In the face of overwhelming English forces supported by the Indians and Loyalists, Governor Rutledge and his City Council were ready to capitulate on not very honorable terms.

This fact made Pulaski so indignant that he broke, in the company of Washington's adjutant, Lt. Colonel Laurens, into the room where negotiations were about to begin. In a strong protest, Casimir

Pulaski authoritatively declared that due to his rank as a Continental officer, he would take the personal responsibility for the defense of Charleston. Negotiations were stopped. British General Prevost was immediately informed of that determination.

The next day, Pulaski sallied out with the Legion which had just arrived. According to his tactics that the best defense is to attack, Pulaski struck first. Hiding the infantry, he arranged a skirmish with the British cavalry. Then, backing up slowly, he led the enemy into a trap with his infantry. In that sortie, the Colonel Kovatch of the legion was killed and officer Zieliński seriously wounded, but the city of Charleston was saved from capitulation. The main forces commanded by General Lincoln soon arrived and forced the enemy to retreat behind the Ashley River.

Now, the British were steadily retreating. Their commander in the South, General Prevost, gave up taking Charleston, then abandoned South Carolina and moved to Georgia. By September 1, 1779, only one base remained, at Savannah, where Prevost had landed a year before.

Meanwhile, the summer's hot days came and Pulaski was still bothered by the unfounded pretensions of the controllers. He was sick and still resided in Charleston. At the beginning of September the French Navy arrived on the coast of Georgia to support the American insurrection.

On September 8, French Admiral Count D'Estaing together with Commanders Rutledge and Lincoln, collaborated on a general plan of siege for the fortified town of Savannah, which was in British hands.

Before the siege of Savannah began on September 16, Count D'Estaing sent a threatening message to General Prevost, asking him to capitulate. The British general played for time and meanwhile British Colonel Maitland with the garrison from Beaufort sneaked into town. The defenses were strengthened tremendously. Consequently Prevost returned the answer to D'Estaing that the town would be defended to the end.

Then, the bombardment of the city began.

SAVANNAH

he town of Savannah containing, at the time, several hundred wooden houses was located at the southern bank of the river of the same name. It was not a fortress, nor a walled city, but was surrounded by a chain of forts protected by moats and a marshy foreground with clumps of trees spreading southward into a forest. Its northern front was protected by the river, and its western side was covered by a thick swamp and wooded tangle. The redoubts and a line of works with abatis and ditches defended the other side. An attack seemed possible only from the southwest side, by the road to Ebezener.

Barely recovered from sickness, Casimir Pulaski, at the forefront of his Legion, arrived at the riverbank of Savannah and established a field camp by Chayton. This way, he was holding up the enemy at the border of Georgia and South Carolina when the American and French forces united to conduct a joint action. The militia from Charleston joined them on September 22, 1779. French warships moved toward the coast at shooting distance.

Trenches were dug and on October 4, the bombardment of the forts and the town began, causing considerable damage to houses within the city and some loss of life, mostly to women, children and blacks. The English commander Prevost requested D'Estaing allow women and children to leave the besieged town, but this was refused after early delays caused by protracted negotiations.

French Admiral D'Estaing worried about his Navy in case of stormy weather. In that light, he urged an immediate attack. Usually prone to quick action, this time Pulaski had a different preconception. He proposed three separate points of attack. Nevertheless, the plan of Admiral D'Estaing and General Lincoln prevailed.

The first 500 American soldiers would demonstratively attack from the west and, in a similar move, so would the French from the south. Gunfire from the sea would panic the town and cause engagement of enemy artillery. Then, the main forces consisting of 2,200 Frenchmen and 1,000 Americans, including Pulaski's Legion, would concentrate in the forest's secret place across the redoubt, Spring Hill. At dawn October 9, the decisive day of the battle, all those forces would launch a deciding storm on the town of Savannah.

Pulaski's Legion was assigned to lead the American light regiments with the task of breaking into enemy lines at the left wing of Spring Hill. Evidently, there was no possibility of action for the cavalry unless the infantry made a large opening.

Pallid stars began vanishing on the firmament, when at 4 a.m. a short distance of one to one-and-a-half miles from the "fortress," one long column of about 4,000 American and French troops were taking their positions at the edge of the forest next to a Jewish cemetery.

The infantry destined to attack Savannah was divided into two groups. At 5:30 a.m. the strong roar of muskets announced a feigned attack by generals Dillon and Huger. They both failed. The main attack was to hit the Spring Hill redoubt. All seemed to be developing as planned.

Admiral D'Estaing with his Frenchmen attacked furiously out of revenge for Quebec and Montreal. It was their big day. In a few moments, the Star Spangled Banner would be blowing over the rampart of Spring Hill. The road to Savannah might have been opened.

Suddenly, things began to go wrong. Amid the murderous fire, they heard the sounds of the enemy's bagpipes. To the astonished D'Estaing, it was a clear sign of the adversary's knowledge about the American-French positions and plans.

"We were betrayed," he wrote later. "The best thing was to make an immediate withdrawal, but we had advanced too far." What was foreseen by the Americans as an easy victory, ended in a disaster due to a treasonous act. Sergeant James Curry, a member of the American force, had secured detailed plans of the attack and had delivered them to British General Prevost.

As a result, the English troops waited in ambush until the attacking insurgents approached to within close shooting range, and being caught by surprise, ran into the deadly fire of the British. In a fierce battle, Admiral D'Estaing, trying to rally the French, fell wounded and the others panicked. Defenders became attackers. Red uniforms and Scottish skirts, in rhythm with their bagpipes, dominated the battlefield. A hail of bullets and the terrible clang of cold weapons aroused hell. Confusion was everywhere because an unrealistic plan of operation had misfired.

The French and American troops passed the abatis and crowded into the ditch, and ascended the berm, while other columns broke away toward the woods under heavy fire from the British ships. Dillon's column got lost in a swamp and emerged in plain view of the British, who promptly opened fire and Dillon retreated.

The cavalry under Pulaski was to precede the American column under Laurens up to the edge of the woods, and then was to wait for an opportunity for action.

The ever-daring Pulaski, however, could not stand patiently by in view of the American retreat. In the midst of heavy smoke and general chaos, he strove, in place of the wounded D'Estaing, to rally the troops and control the situation. Casimir realized the failure. What to do next? He was sorry for the Legion. However, it was not his fault. This was not his plan nor decision. It was not his overall command either, but withdrawal now would cause extreme losses. Casimir decided to save the situation as much as he could and tried to do his best.

With a raised sword, at the head of 200 horsemen, he pointed toward Spring Hill and shouted: "Hurray! Forward! Naprzód!" His legionnaires in full gallop jumped bravely to counterattack. Enraged, Pulaski desperately pushed forward when D'Estaing was taking redoubt Ebenezer, also called Spring Hill. When Casimir's horse fell dead, he was hit in the right thigh, but still was giving commands: "Go ahead and follow the Uhlans, I told them to attack," he screamed to Colonel Horry, to whom he turned over the command of the cavalry. Then Horry immediately charged with full power, and Casimir galloped to the French lines and was wounded twice.

Unfortunately, all that was in vain. While changing horses, Pulaski was shot and mortally wounded. His soldiers carried him, badly bleeding, away from the battlefield. It is probable that Casimir had two friends close to him at his last moments: Maurycy Beniowski and Felix Miklaszewicz. The Savannah engagement was abandoned by the allied armies.

Doctor James Lynah operated on Pulaski right away. He removed the grapeshot bullet from Casimir's groin. The surgery weakened the patient. High fever came, indicative of infection. Very sick, Casimir Pulaski was taken to the brig "Wasp." He hallucinated. On regaining consciousness he knew that he was going to die. He asked to notify Generals Washington and LaFayette about what had happened and complained about not being able to see Poland anymore.

Casimir Pulaski's life ended a few days after receiving the wound on October 9, 1779. "It was a great loss for the American cause," commented General D'Estaing. "Pulaski tried to penetrate beyond the enemy's broken line when he was wounded."

Because there is no firm and unanimous evidence about his burial as well as about the battle scene, some historians claimed that, according to the naval custom, his dead body was "buried at sea"— meaning that Pulaski had a seaman's funeral. That could be questioned, since the "Wasp," enroute to Charleston, never lost sight of the land to make a sea burial necessary.

In 1853, Philadelphia's "Herald" published an interesting story about Pulaski's death as related by Dr. James Lynah's grandson. Grandfather Lynah as an old man used to tell him about the surgery he performed on General Pulaski at Savannah. He claimed that Count Pulaski had a chance of survival, if he agreed to be carried on stretchers with the American army and stay under Dr. Lynah's care. However, Pulaski opposed the idea for fear that he might fall into English hands. His greatest fear was that the British might have put him into the hands of his enemy, the Russians. Rather than that, Casimir preferred to die on an American ship.

Presumably, Pulaski's body was transferred to land by a small naval boat. Then, Casimir was quickly buried in the village of Greenwich near Savannah. On October 21, 1779, the symbolic ceremony in Charleston took place. It was, first, to honor the hero, and, secondly, to stop the British from searching for his body that they might have traded to the Russians for a big reward.

Casimir Pulaski's funeral took place in Charleston in the military manner. Three American and three French officers carried the mourning shroud and Star Spangled Banner. A brisk steed in full armor was led and the uniform of the hero named "Count Casimir (Kazimierz) Pulaski, Brigadier-General of the American Cavalry" was displayed. Next, marched survivors of the Legion, not numerous. Admiral D'Estaing, with his wounded hand in a sling, led French soldiers under their banner of lilies. Farther on, walked soldiers of the American insurrectionist army, followed by a crowd of civilians.

The sympathetic, age-honored General Benjamin Lincoln served as the Herald officer of the final call. The names of battles fought for American Independence were announced publicly:

Brandywine
Germantown
Cooper's Ferry
Egg Harbor
Charleston
Savannah

"The hero perished on the field of glory! Forever be praised his name."

Many a soldier, hardened in battles, who day by day lived near death, repeated these words with touching emotion and discreetly brushed a tear, particularly when a military chaplain delivered a patriotic address.

Pulaski's death sowed flowers of legend and hero-worship began.

A Lasting Legacy

PASSWORD "PULASKI"
COUNTERSIGN "POLAND"

ommander-in-Chief George Washington received the fallen hero's saber and on November 17, 1779, he assigned that the day's password "Pulaski" would have the countersign "Poland." That reciprocal linkage echoed through over two centuries.

On November 22, 1779, Congress passed a resolution to build a monument in memory of General Count Casimir Pulaski in Savannah. In 1825, Marquis de LaFayette, the French statesman and hero of the American War for Independence, was in Savannah to lay a cornerstone for the monument, containing a time capsule. When 29 years later, in 1854, the marble and granite monument was unveiled, it was at a new place. The capsule was moved there and sealed in the base together with a new cornerstone capsule containing medals, newspapers and about 50 other items, along with an urn believed (and disbelieved) to hold Pulaski's remains.

With no clear indications on the monument plaques, controversies over Casimir Pulaski's burial place persisted for over a century. In 1996, the the Polish American researcher Edward Pinkowski (he had the support of the principal author of this book, Antoni Lenkiewicz) lent support to the idea that Pulaski's remains have been left resting in peace under Robert Launitz's column in Monterey Square in Savannah.

The monument weights 20 tons. Marble slabs, cemented block by block, rise up like a tapered arrow to the height of 55 feet, with a Lady of Liberty holding a wreath of glory on its top.

Today, in the beautiful city of Savannah, many places commemorate the Polish-American hero and his legacy spread over the entire

United States of America. In 1867, the U.S. Congress acquired a bust of Casimir Pulaski by sculptor Henry Dmochowski vel Saunders for the Capitol Building. In 1910, an equestrian statue was erected in Washington, D.C. Pulaski's monuments are scattered across the United States. They are to be found in Utica, N.Y.; Milwaukee, Wisc.; Baltimore, Md.; Detroit, Mich.; Philadelphia, Pa.; and many other towns and cities. There are nearly 30 cities and counties bearing the name "Pulaski." Numerous parks, streets, bridges, highways, schools, etc. bear the name "Pulaski." Hundreds of organizations, clubs, foundations, associations function under "Pulaski's" patronage. Apart from those, some 21,000 Pulaski listings in the U.S. telephone directories prove the popularity of his Polish name.

"Pulaski Day" is a permanent holiday in Chicago, celebrated in March (first Monday), and annually proclaimed by the executive branches of states and cities all over the United States of America and celebrated by Americans of Polish descent and all those who appreciate the Polish hero's contribution to the American independence.

Many American presidents recognized Casimir Pulaski as a man of valor and courage and a builder of a bridge of alliance between the two continents. True, many have done so with an eye toward their Polish electorate. It does not come as a surprise that in their official pronouncements Presidents Taft, Hoover, Kennedy and Carter addressed different aspects from those stressed by Reagan, Bush and Clinton. In his Pulaski Day proclamation in 1982, President Ronald Reagan particularly hit a nerve when he stressed, at the crucial time for the world, that the Polish-American hero struggled not only for our mutually held ideals but also against the mutual enemy.

To the password "Pulaski"—the countersign is "Poland," and that has remained unchanged. Our solemn duty is to observe that motto by better understanding the ways that led Casimir Pulaski to his immortal fame and Poland to become a strategic ally of the USA in Europe.

BURIAL and BODY IDENTIFICATION

*A*n independent researcher, Mr. Edward Pinkowski dedicated many years and much energy and scientific zeal, to verify the circumstances of Casimir Pulaski's death and burial. He dug through the archives and queried various sources to counter the once prevailing thesis of Pulaski's burial at sea, long suspecting the maritime tradition to be apocryphal.

His research proved that the badly wounded Pulaski was one of the last two hospital cases onboard the private schooner "Wasp," mentioned in the ship log. The schooner was at that time stationed at Thunderbolt Bluff and pressed to service to evacuate artillery guns and transport the sick and wounded from Savannah to Charleston, South Carolina.

At that time, Captain Bulfinch commanding this hospital ship, had no more room to take aboard passengers and denied admission to another wounded soldier, Lieutenant Van Vheland. Vheland must have applied prior to Pulaski's death. Otherwise, Pulaski's death would have created a vacancy aboard the "Wasp" making his admission possible. Pinkowski learned from another source that a coffin was made for Pulaski by a "Wasp" crewmember, Eleaser Phillips. His widow later requested a widow's benefit from the government.

As was customary, Pulaski was buried in his military uniform with a flag draped over the body. His burial took place on the Greenwich plantation across the road from the present Bonaventure Cemetery. Until December 1853, the body was buried on the scenic bank of a creek emptying into the Savannah River. At that time, Major William P. Bowen, a grandson to the original plantation owner, opened the grave and, as a member of the Pulaski Monument Committee, placed the iron box with the remains in the brick vault beneath the monument. By placing the box under the monument in Savannah's Monterey Square he hoped to rescue the remains from oblivion.

In a continuous effort at authenticating the discovery of Pulaski's remains, DNA tests have been carried out. A DNA sample was taken of remaining teeth. The right hand was x-rayed since it had been well known and recorded that, during his Confederacy period, after he had been ambushed by the Russians at Grab on January 13, 1770, Pulaski had been wounded and for some time was unable to write and had to dictate his letters. Pinkowski also noticed an imprint on Casimir's collarbone made by a metal medallion, a good luck gift from Princess Francesca, which he was known to wear.

Several years ago, a truly sensational discovery was made in Savannah during the restoration of the Pulaski monument. The removal of the obelisque opened access to an underground vault yielding an iron container with human remains with Pulaski's name inscribed on its cover. Mr. Edward Pinkowski whose studies alerted the city authorities to that possibility scored a major discovery.

It has been most encouraging to see that fundamental biographical data can be set straight some two hundred years later.

TRANSLATOR'S REMARKS

$\mathcal{T}$he original version of Antoni Lenkiewicz's book, entitled "Kazimierz Pulaski (1745-1779)," is written in his rich idiomatic Polish and is not easily adaptable into English. The translator's task was further complicated by the fact that the author's often idiosyncratic views and opinions required further clarification to make them understandable to readers not well versed in Polish history and culture.

Readers familiar with the Polish language are advised to turn to the original work. This version is a mere adaptation for our American readers. With the author's permission, I have re-arranged chapters and amended the text, consulting other sources to describe the sad period of Polish history in the 18th century.

There are many books on Casimir Pulaski, in Polish and English. They seem to fall into two categories. They are either fictionalized or are of scholarly and documentary value. Lenkiewicz's book is unique in the way it combines both characteristics. It is both a popular, almost fictional work for pleasurable pursuit and, at the same time, a sound work of history. Such a work has long been missing from bookstore and library shelves. I feel honored that the task has fallen to me to make the book accessible to American readers and thank the author for acknowledging my contribution as a co-author.

Ted Kwiatkowski, San Diego, California

Translator's Words to Ponder

"Confederacy" vs. "Confederation"

"Confederacy" means alliance, league, coalition, union, or an association, as of nations, for a common goal and over matters of superior rank and value. "Confederation" applies mostly to private business associations, a little beneath the rank of Confederacy.

"Generality" vs. "Generalcy"
"Generality" means the quality or state of being general in a broad sense. "Generalcy" describes position or function of a person, an office or a term of a general.

HISTORIC TERMS

„For Your Freedom and Ours"

Adam Mickiewicz, Polish national poet, was to sum up the sizeable tradition when in 1833 he declared from exile in Paris: „Whenever there is a struggle for Freedom there is also a struggle for Poland".

Mickiewicz credited historian Joachim Lelewel with putting this slogan on Polish revolutionary banners. Casimir Pulaski was the precursor of the idea first spread by the Polish legionnaires in Napoleon's army wearing on their sleeves the embroidered inscription: „Free people are our brothers." The idea dominated the Polish democratic political thought from the last partition in 1795 to the rebirth of the 2nd Republic in 1918. This expression of Polish solidarity with the oppressed developed during the 1931 Uprising against the Tsarist government and in solidarity with the Russian people, who suffered under the same yoke of despotism.

Polish Republic or Commonwealth

Poland proper and the Duchy of Lithuania (embracing also the Ukraine and Byelorussia) merged in 1383 under the Jagiellon dynasty through the marriage of the Lithuanian Duke Jagiello (Jogaila) and the Polish Queen Jadwiga of the Anjou and Piast lines.

Limited monarchy under the Jagiellons led, with the extinction of the dynasty, to the period of **electoral monarchy,** the kings' executive power tempered by the legislative power vested in the Seym.

Courland

Courland was a fiefdom of Poland. Prince Karol (1733-1796) was the son of the then Polish king, Augustus III, of the Saxon House of Wettin, the dynasty now on the British throne. He received Kettler's crown in 1759, becoming Courland's regent. The crown was named after Ferdinand Kettler (1655-1737), the last Grand Master of the Livonian Knights or Brothers of the Sword who, after the order got secularized, became the first regent of the fiefdoms of Courland and Semigalia and governed the dukedoms for the Polish king. Some Bar confederates favored Karol's candidacy for the Polish elective throne.

Sublime Porte

The Sultan's court and a complex of palaces in Istanbul, representing the Ottoman Empire, as the White House stands for the United States of America.

Count Pulaski

Strictly speaking, the Pulaski family did not have the title of Count since no such title, by law, existed in Poland. However, used abroad, it served well to describe the stature and position of the family, and was useful in America. In the title-hungry America, during the Revolutionary War, Pulaski used it as expediency.

Marshal of Łomża

The Marshal of Łomża was a title of one regional commander. Some publications have referred to Pulaski as a „Marshal of Poland." This is in error. Only the Polish king had the authority to name a marshal of the country as only the king had the power to call the „levy en mass" („pospolite ruszenie") or conscription.

Hetman – Captain, Commander

Starosta – District Magistrate or Elder

Voivode and Voivodeship

From Old Polish 'voj' nmeaning 'soldier' and 'vod' – root of 'wodzić'—'to lead,' the words originally meant, respectively, a military leader and his area of command. In modern usage, 'wojewoda' ('voivode') is a leader of a large administrative unit and 'voivodeship' is the unit.

GENERAL READING MATTER

Brzoza, Jan "Kazimierz Pułaski." Warszawa 1960.

Collins, David R. "Casimir Pulaski. A Soldier on Horseback". Gretna, Louisiana: Pelikan, 1997.

Davies, Norman, "God's Playground. A History of Poland." Vol. 1-2. New York: Columbia Univ. Press, 1982.

Haiman, Miecislaus, "Kosciuszko in the American Revolution." New York: PIASA, 1943.

Halecki, Oskar, "A History of Poland." New York: D.MacKay Co., 1976.

Kajencki, Francis Casimir, "Casimir Pulaski, Cavalry Commander of the American Revolution." El Paso: Southwest Polonia Press, 2001.

Konopczynski, Władysław, "Casimir Pulaski." Transl. Irena Makarewicz. Chicago: Polish Roman Catholic Union of America, 1947.

Lossing, Benson J. "The Pictorial Field-Book of the Revolution." New York, 1851-1852.

Manning, Clarence A. "Soldier of Liberty. Casimir Pulaski," New York 1945.

Olszer, Krystyna, "For Your Freedom and Ours. Polish Progressive Spirit from the 14th Century to the Present." New York: Ungar Publ., 1981.

Roszko, Janusz, "Ostatni rycerz Europy." Katowice 1983.

Sparks, Jared, "Count Pulaski" in: "The Library of American Biography." Vol. 15, Boston 1845.

Sulek, Zdzisław, "Polacy w wojnie o niepodległość Stanów Zjednoczonych 1775-1783." Warszawa 1976.

Szymanski, Leszek, "Casimir Pulaski. A Hero of the American Revolution. New York: Hippocrene Books, Inc., 1994.

PULASKI MOVIE IN THE WORKS

𝒯he 225th anniversary of Pulaski's demise spurred interest in producing the movie on the hero. Andrzej Pastuszek, a great talent lost to the Polish culture by his emigration in 1981, came out of nowhere in 1998 with a film concept, "Field of Blood." He produced an inspired scenario and, with an unusual practicality, organized his own Pulaski Film Production Company selling shares, and in 1997 began negotiating with Tadeusz Ścibor-Rylski, chief of the Polish Cinematography.

By 1997, Leszek Szymanski, from California, already copyrighted his complete "Pulaski" screenplay, and started circulating it within the industry. Szymanski's screenplay is an offshoot of his 1994 monographic study and enabled him to pursue his insights into Pulaski's life and personality gained when working on his scholarly work. The "Pulaski" screenplay brings into play the author's experience and viewpoint as an immigrant.

When these huge and costly proposals fell through, "Kontakt" came out with a modest but workable proposal of making a documentary on Pulaski as the 225th anniversary project. Jolanta Kessler-Chojecka's screenplay, revised serveral times since 2001, is in the works. Her film will interview a number of Pulaski scholars and survey the rich artifacts from Pulaski's period kept in Warka and other Polish museums.

Regina Gorzkowska-Rossi

INDEX

POŁOCK

WITEBSK

GDAŃSK

WILNO

AUGUSTÓW

GRODNO

BYDGOSZCZ

NOWOGRÓDEK

MIŃSK

MOHYLEW

ŁOMŻA

POZNAŃ   OSTROŁĘKA   BIAŁYSTOK

BARANOWICZE

WARSZAWA

CZECZERSK

BRZEŚĆ

PINSK

WIELUŃ

MOZYRZ

CZĘSTOCHOWA   KOWEL

CZARNOBYL

ZAMOŚĆ

ŁUCK

KRAKÓW

LWÓW

POŁONNE   ŻYTOMIERZ

KAMIENIEC

BERDYCZÓW

PODOLSKI

HUMAŃ

STRYJ

BAR

ZWANIEC   TARGOWICA

100 km

Poland 1770

Casimir Pulaski's battle trail in America, July 23, 1777 to October 11, 1779.
After Zdzisław Sułek, "Polacy w wojnie o niepodległość Stanów Zjednoczonych
1775-1783" (Warszawa 1976).

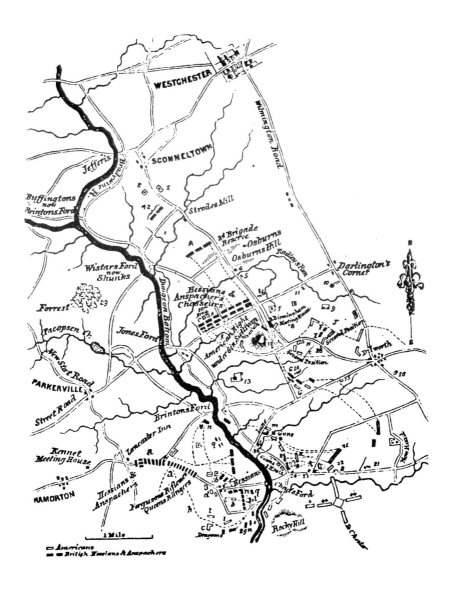

Battle of Brandywine, Sept. 11, 1777. Taken from "The Pictorial Field-Book of
the Revolution" by Benson J. Lossing (1860).

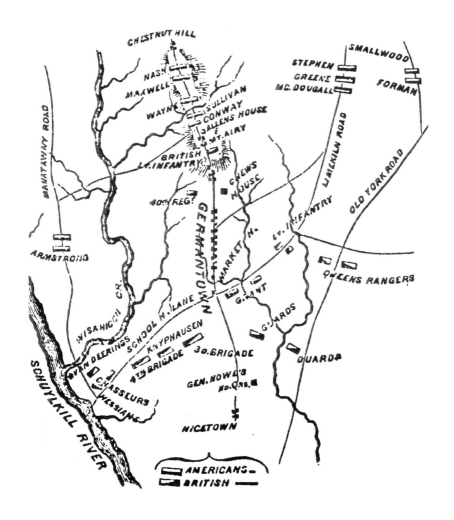

Battle of Germantown, October, 1777. Taken from "The Pictorial Field-Book of the Revolution" by Benson J. Lossing (1860).

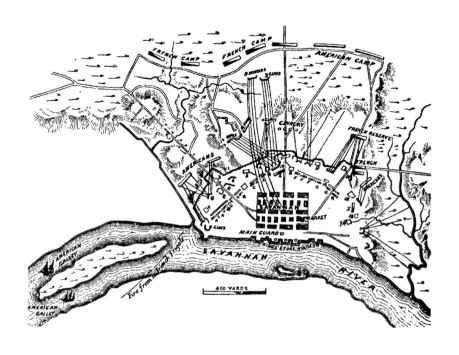

Siege of Savannah, Oct. 9, 1779. Taken from "The Pictorial Field-Book of the Revolution" by Benson J. Lossing (1860).

Group portrait of Bar confederates with Casimir Pulaski in the centher, they are, clockwise, Prince Michał Ogiński, hetman of Lithuania; Reverend Marek Jandołowicz, Joseph Miączyński, Marshal of Bełżec; Gen. Charles Francois Dumouriez; Maurycy Beniowski; Marcin Oracewicz, Cracow landowner; Francis Kellerman, Marshal of France; and French General Baron Anthony-Charles Vioménil. It first appeared in the 1899 "Album" by S. Wolski and is a clear indication how posterity appraised Casimir's role as a Confederacy leader. (Reprinted in J. S. Kopczewski's "Kosciuszko and Pulaski.")

Joseph Pulaski (1704-1769), Casimir's Father. Unknown painter.
After Władysław Konopczyński's "Kazimierz Pułaski" (Kraków 1931).

Karol Wettin, Prince of Courland.
By an unknown artist.

Francesca, née Krasińska,
Princess of Courland. By M. Stein.
Printed after Władysław Konopczyński's
"Kazimierz Pułaski," (Kraków 1931).

Casimir Pulaski and Confederates by Częstochowa. Oil by Juliusz Kossak.